White Angel

A Journey In Her Own Words
The Personal Memoirs of Helen Weinberg
1914-1997

P'NINA SEPLOWITZ

with Rabbi Dr. Noam Weinberg

Order this book online at www.trafford.com
or email orders@trafford.com

Most Trafford titles are also available at major online book retailers.

Printed in the United States of America.

ISBN: 978-1-4669-8557-5 (sc)
ISBN: 978-1-4669-8559-9 (hc)
ISBN: 978-1-4669-8558-2 (e)

Library of Congress Control Number: 2013904591

Trafford rev. 10/01/2013

 www.trafford.com

North America & international
toll-free: 1 888 232 4444 (USA & Canada)
fax: 812 355 4082

ACKNOWLEDGEMENTS

I wish to express my deepest gratitude to God, for enabling me to accomplish this most fulfilling task.

There have been many individuals who have contributed to the preparation of this book. Special thanks to my parents, Bernard and Eileen Weinberg, and to my Uncle Aaron and Aunt Susan Weinberg, for their support and contributions to this book. Thank you to Naftali Ejdelman from Yiddish Farm, Rivka Schiller and Gosha Wozniak for your impeccable translations. Thank you to my brother Noam Weinberg without whose assistance, hours of devotion and incredible memory, I would not have been able to complete this book, and of course to his wife, Nechama, for her patience throughout this project. Thank you to my sister and best friend Dena for always being there for me. Finally, thank you to my husband James who has been a tremendous source of support and encouragement for this project. I am indebted to you for always letting me follow my dreams.

DEDICATION

This book is dedicated in honor of all the Holocaust survivors who waged the battle of their lives with dignity, strength, resilience and belief, inspiring subsequent generations and paving the way for the future of the Jewish people.

When compiling this book, I found a piece of paper on which my grandmother had written the following proverb attributed to the saintly Rabbi Yohanan ben Zakkai, a first century tannaic leader: *"A nation, however strong, cannot live long with physical strength alone."* Although the Nazis destroyed one-third of the world's Jewish population, it is this deep-rooted spiritual strength that has enabled the perseverance of the Jewish people.

P'nina Seplowitz

CONTENTS

AUTHOR'S NOTE   xi

FOREWORD   xiii

TIMELINE   xvii

INTRODUCTION   xix

Chapter One   MY NIGHTMARE BEGINS   1

Chapter Two   IN MY OLD HOME - IN MAYN ALTER HEYM   3

Chapter Three   THE MATURA   11

Chapter Four   WHITE ANGELS   17

Chapter Five   WORLD WAR TWO   23

Chapter Six   THE ESCAPE   27

Chapter Seven   BARUCH CHAIM   35

Chapter Eight   AARON ASHER   41

Chapter Nine   THE LAND OF THE FREE   55

Chapter Ten   WHAT IS HAPPINESS   69

Chapter Eleven   I CANNOT FORGET YOU, MY KREMENITZ   71

Chapter Twelve   A POETIC TRIBUTE TO KREMENITZ   75

Chapter Thirteen   ROKHELEH   81

Chapter Fourteen   FOREVER MY JERUSALEM   87

Chapter Fifteen   ROUGH TIMES   97

Chapter Sixteen   WORDS ARE NO LONGER ENOUGH   103

Addendum   ASSORTED POETRY   111

AUTHOR'S NOTE

In a dusty box hidden in a corner of my parents' garage I found a treasure that finally pieced together the puzzle of my grandmother's life, her sorrow and her dreams. Inside that box were many pages of history written by my grandmother, a Holocaust survivor. Who knew she was even a writer? When I sifted through the worn yellow pages, some in Yiddish, some in Polish and some in English - a deep chill ran down my spine. *Bobby*,[1] the grandmother I knew and admired for her brilliance and myriad of talents, such as cooking, sewing and knitting, had a secret. An awful and violent nightmare that she kept tucked away and never let out. These newly discovered stories, essays and poetry provided a window into her soul.

I decided that the story of my grandmother had to be told and what better way than to use her words as a guide through the different periods of her life. After having her Yiddish and Polish writings translated, I came to realize that many of her experiences were simply too difficult for her to bear, so she recounted these events through seemingly fictional stories, such as the one entitled "Rokheleh." Other times it was her poetry that she used as a vehicle for self-expression. There were specific themes and imagery that were repetitious throughout her writing and provided a deeper insight into her struggles and dreams.

I am both proud and humbled to present the story of my grandmother, the plight of a young woman who was separated from

---

[1] The endearing term we used to reference our grandmother in Yiddish, often pronounced *Bubbe*.

her family during World War Two, imprisoned, beaten, starved and tortured. Yet, despite it all, she was able to search into the depths of her hope and faith in God and find an inner strength to survive. I always saw my *Bobby* as a fragile woman, a soft-spoken underdog, the one who aimed to please. Not the fighter, the warrior or the heroine that she was. If only I knew her full story while she was alive, I would have asked her so many questions. But, it is no coincidence that this treasure box came to light only after her death. In my adulthood, as I am raising a family of my own, it is evident that the similarities between us are uncanny. Our neatness and organizational skills, devotion to our children, love for writing and our ability to hope and dream tie us together. Without my grandmother's hopes and dreams, I may never have been blessed to even enter this world at all.

There was no question that it was my duty to transcribe her words and tell her story. I am exceptionally grateful to my brother, Noam, whose vivid recollections of conversations he had with our grandmother added so much to this book. The life of my *Bobby* patterns the lives of so many others who experienced the Holocaust. Each survivor has a story to tell and each story is unique in its own right. However, many Holocaust memoirs retell the story as a narrative from the point of view of the survivor. My *Bobby* was not capable of doing that. She could not speak of her struggles and despair. Rather, she painted a picture of what was lost through her poetry and secret journal. Many survivors were cunning and daring, physically fighting odds to keep themselves alive. *Bobby* went to a place deep in her mind, perhaps as she lay on the damp floors of the Soviet jails, or in the dead of winter in a Siberian hard labor camp and imagined a time of great hope. This gave her the strength to push on. Her themes of spring and sun which are depicted in almost everything she wrote are her way of bemoaning and longing for a past that does not exist anymore. What makes the story of Helen Weinberg nee Gun unique is that her actual written story of survival is the inextricable force that helped her survive.

In order to distinguish between my grandmother's words and my own, I have used two different fonts throughout the book.

FOREWORD

By Rabbi Dr. Noam Weinberg

I echo the aforementioned words of my sister when I say that the story of my grandmother is not an exclusive one. It is just one of the thousands of stories of survival through the darkest period in human history that the world has ever known. One young woman's lost world, forgotten forever, has been recreated only through dreams and stories. But her story is unique to us, me and my sister, and, indeed, to our entire family. Helen Weinberg's story of survival is our story. It is the reason why we exist today. It is the motivation behind my passion for this project and why I am so indebted to my sister for taking the lead on this important work.

Our dedication to seeing this through to completion stands as a testament to the love, respect and admiration that we will always have for our grandmother. It should be made clear, however, that this story is not one for our family alone; rather, it is a significant historical work intended for those who are searching for inspiration as well as for students of Holocaust studies.

My grandmother's world was shattered by her experiences during the war. Her only hope was to try and pick up the pieces and put them back together in a way that resembled a normal existence at a time well before the trend of seeking mental health assistance from a professional. She married my grandfather whose experiences were also difficult as he lived with memories of the war, his own incarceration in a Soviet slave labor camp and the knowledge that almost everyone that he knew and loved was exterminated.

The story of how my grandparents met, had it not been for such pathetic circumstances, would have been the making of a Hollywood romance. My grandfather, a young Hassidic man, suffered from a hernia which required surgery. While recovering in the Jewish hospital in Krakow he was tended to by a pretty, young nurse by the name of Helen Gun from the town of Kremenitz. Later, after their liberation from the hell of the Siberian labor camps, my grandfather from Novo Sibirsk, and my grandmother from Arkhangelsk, the repatriated Poles were taken down to Uzbekistan by train where they were given temporary reprieve. On one such train, my grandfather noticed a familiar looking young woman. After talking for a few minutes, they realized that it was my grandmother who had served as my grandfather's nurse in Krakow a few years earlier. Their courtship was quick and they married on January 1, 1942.

After reading through her journals, both my sister and I recognized that while we thought our grandmother was incapable of expressing her emotions, in fact she was, just not through direct conversation. The pen and paper were her catharsis for the emotional torture she endured each day. She wrote down some of her memoirs; however, the majority of her writing was conscious streams of thought, which she fashioned into short stories or poetry. As opposed to most biographies or autobiographies which are told as a story of factual occurrences, what makes Helen Weinberg's narrative so distinctive is the way in which it is told: through her own words.

When I would spend time with my grandparents I often encouraged them to talk about their experiences. Usually it ended with my grandmother crying. On holidays when the *Yizkor*[2] prayer was said, I remember seeing my grandparents cry, unable to speak about the horrors of their past. And when I would sleep at their home, I would hear them mutter and moan at night, reliving experiences and dealing with the nightmares. Watching my grandparents as a child, I noticed they slept with their hands tucked under their heads, conditioned from years without a pillow in the labor camps. We were not allowed to buy German products, another overt scar from the trauma they endured. But my memories also include the gentle

---

[2]   A special memorial prayer said on specific holidays throughout the Jewish calendar.

grandmother who loved us unconditionally. She fed us when we were hungry, basked in the smiles on our faces when she gave us chocolate candy and truly enjoyed our company.

Our grandmother was a brilliant woman who was constantly learning and growing while serving as a devoted wife, mother, and grandmother. In Europe, my grandmother was granted admission to the local gymnasium due to her intelligence and enthusiasm for learning. She survived the destruction of European Jewry and emerged from the ashes of the Holocaust with her sense of dignity and pride. The last time I saw my grandmother, she was lying in bed in her home, with labored breathing and a weak pulse. She called me over and asked me a question. "When is *Moshiach*[3] coming?" I had no answer, but I assured her it would be soon. Then she said, "Please promise me that you will get a doctorate." And so years later when I received my doctorate, there was no question that it would be dedicated to my grandmother for all that she represented in life and in memory.

On the morning of my doctoral defense, I was clearing my head in the Gottesman Library at Yeshiva University. I decided to go to the fourth floor and look around at the old books on display. Moments before it was time for me to go to the actual defense, I walked over to a random bookshelf. In front of me was a copy of a memory book called *Pinkas Kremenitz* written by survivors from the town of Kremenitz, where my grandmother grew up. I knew that my grandmother had written some poems in several other memory books but I had never seen this one. When I opened up the memory book, I was shocked to find I was staring at one of my grandmother's poems! I like to think she was letting me know that she was with me then just as she always was in life.

I pray that this book serves as a testament to all that she went through and accomplished, the hardships and the tribulations. But, most of all, this book will enable us to always remember *Bobby*.

---

3   The Jewish Messiah.

TIMELINE

1906 - Rochele Kalton from Odessa marries Baruch Chaim Gun

April 1, 1914 - Lena (Helen) Gun is born

1927 - Helen Gun, age 13, prepares for the Matura Exam

1934-1939 - Helen Gun attends Nursing School in Krakow, Poland

1935 - Yaakov (Kuba) Gun, the only son, leaves Kremenitz with his wife Elza and moves to Tel Aviv

September 22, 1939 - Soviet authorities take over Kremenitz, which was previously part of Poland

1940 - Helen Gun escapes German occupied Poland, is captured by the Soviets and sent to prison for 18 months and subsequently to a Siberian labor camp

January 1, 1942 - Helen Gun marries Yaakov Weinberg in Uzbekistan

November 16, 1944 - Baruch Chaim (Bernard), first child, is born in Samarkand

May 8, 1945 - World War Two ends and family is displaced

1946 - Helen, Jack and Bernard settle in the American DP camp in Ulm, Germany

July, 1947 - Denied entry to board the illegal ship "Exodus" to Palestine

July 16, 1947 - Aaron Asher (Aaron), second child, is born in Ulm, Germany

November 24, 1949 (Thanksgiving Day) - Weinberg family arrives in New York Harbor

June, 1963 - Helen Weinberg takes her first trip to Israel

April 14, 1967 - Kuba Gun, Helen's only living sibling passes away

June 29, 1971 - Bernard Weinberg and Eileen Graber are married

August 11, 1971 - Aaron Weinberg and Susan Fisher are married

September 28, 1997 - Beloved Helen Weinberg passes away

INTRODUCTION

Helen Weinberg, nee Gun, grew up on the outskirts of the ancient town of Kremenitz. Kremenitz, one of the oldest cities in Poland, is rich with Jewish heritage and history. The first mention of Jews in Kremenitz was in the year 1438, when the Grand Duke of Lithuania gave them a charter. Such charters, or laws, were important because they decreed that the Jewish population formed a class of free citizens who lived under the protection of the Grand Duke and his local administration.

Helen's mother, Rochele, nee Kalton, hailed from the Russian town of Odessa and married Baruch Chaim Gun circa 1900. They resided in Kremenitz where Baruch was a watch and clock repairman. He was poor and shared a home with his sister and her husband, the Zaltz family. Yosef Zaltz, who was a first cousin to Helen, grew up in the Gun home in Kremenitz and was like a brother to her and her sisters. He married Manya Feur in Germany after World War Two and moved to Israel. They settled in Acco where he taught Hebrew before being promoted to principal of the local elementary school. Yosef had a lively personality and loved to sing. In the early 1950s, when the First Lady Eleanor Roosevelt came to Israel, Yosef invited her to his home and she accepted!

The etymology of the last name Gun has two distinct meanings according to our family tradition. Although spelled differently, there are those who maintain that it comes from the word "*Gaon*" which means genius, and was a name given to the family to honor their outstanding intellectual abilities. This was what our grandmother always shared with us. The other tradition is that since the "G"

and "H" are interchangeable in Russian, the name suggests that a segment of the family line came from the Jewish Huns who lived in Europe until about the sixth century. The family was traditional, neither Hassidic nor Lithuanian in practice, although Helen's dialect of Yiddish was closer to the Hassidic style. They were considered enlightened and placed secular education in high regard.

Rochele and Baruch were blessed with four children: Roza, Sara, Yaakov (Kuba), and Lena (Helen).[4] Roza was born in 1905. She married Mundik Zeeman and studied to be a nurse. Sara, born in 1907, was a homemaker and married Ze'ev (Wowa) Gitelman who worked as a locksmith. They had one child, a daughter named Shoshana (Sosia). On August 12, 1942, Ukrainian and German members of the Einsatzgruppen killed Roza, Mundik, Sara, Wowa and four-year-old Sosia and they were buried in a mass grave.

Baruch Chaim and Rochele Gun

---

4   Helen was given the name Yenta at birth.

Roza and Helen

Mundik and Roza Zeeman

Sarah in a veiled hat, newly married
with husband Wowa Gitelman

Helen, Roza and Sara

Yaakov, or Kuba, Gun was the only son born to Rochele and Boruch. As a young Socialist Zionist, his heart was set on re-building the Jewish ancient homeland in Palestine. In the early 1930s he married a young woman by the name of Aliza Lingel (Elza) who shared his dream of *aliyah*.[5] They left Kremenitz in 1935 and moved to Tel Aviv. Kuba studied law in Poland and worked for the electric company in Haifa. Elza was a comptroller for Shekem department stores.

Kuba and Helen

---

[5] Literally meaning "going up", it is a term used to denote individuals who move to Israel.

Gun family photo circa 1930; Helen is on bottom right

Helen, first from left, in Kremenitz

Helen, affectionately known as Lena, was the youngest daughter. Her early life was spent as a student of culture and academics. She excelled at her studies and was part of a very warm and close family structure. Kremenitz had a quota for young Jewish girls in the local public school or gymnasium. However, due to Helen's exceptional skills, knowledge base, and ability to quickly understand and assimilate information, she was admitted into the gymnasium. In addition to her fond memories of school, our grandmother would often talk longingly of the austere beauty of her hometown of Kremenitz. She used to tell us stories of frolicking in the forest with friends to pick fresh berries from which her mother made jams and wine. She would talk about the underground cellar which kept the food cool in the warm summers. There were hanging spices and pickled vegetables which adorned the cellar. Everything was processed by hand and taught to her by her mother. Kremenitz was her playground, it was her school, and it was her lifeblood. Attached to the land that nourished her as it had her parents before her, the war ripped it from her as if tearing out her heart. In her own words . . .

Chapter One

MY NIGHTMARE BEGINS

From The Journal of Helen Weinberg 1969

There was a war, a terrible war which will be written with bloody letters in the pages of world history. Will it be forgotten? Not for a very long time as too many people suffered and too much human blood was spilled. An extreme case of human tragedy cannot be erased from one's heart and memory. This immense tragedy concerned the Jewish people in particular.

It is not a fairy tale or a fantasy, which can be used as a subject for a novel or a motion picture. It is the truth and it occurred in our time when we were the victims and lived through a personal tragedy. Hours and hours can be spent telling its story, and although the stories are different, the sufferings are much alike.

We all attempt to forget those memories in order to continue our lives. The Almighty spared our lives and we became the lucky ones to have a little time to enjoy this beautiful world. Now we have to force ourselves to collect all the possible strength that is left in us and, from broken pieces, rebuild a new life. But, it is very hard to forget the past no matter how much we try because our memories do not allow us.

Like many others, I also was a victim of that terrible war called World War Two. I was caught in it in my blooming years of youth when I began to see life's pleasures. When the war broke out on

September 1, 1939 I was in Krakow, Poland, where I worked as a registered nurse.

I came to Krakow from a small town in Poland called Kremenitz where I was born in 1914 and raised in a family of three sisters and one brother. My family was part of the Haskalah, the Jewish Enlightenment. We were educated in secular studies, Hebrew language, and Jewish history. After high school graduation, I left my hometown to continue my education. My love for people and my desire to help those who were suffering led me to choose the profession of nursing. It is well known that this profession requires hard work and a great deal of patience. It was much harder than today's training for professional nursing, which included six days a week and twelve hours a day. I was happy with my work and tried to give as much devotion and love as possible to the sick and I was repaid with the great feeling and appreciation for helping them. After graduation from nursing school, I remained working in the same hospital where I had done my training.

At the outbreak of the war, I found myself working with very ill patients. I felt I had the responsibility to stay and help the sick, so I didn't leave Krakow despite the fact that my entire family was still in my hometown of Kremenitz. It is very important to be united with dear ones especially in times of war and disasters. I saw people running away leaving behind their homes and belongings to escape the bombings and killings. When the Germans occupied Krakow they began robbing stores and forcing people into hard work. But worst of all was the persecution and torture of Jews that is so well known to the world.

| Chapter Two |

IN MY OLD HOME -
IN MAYN ALTER HEYM

Kremenitz 1914

A dark morning covered the walls. Heavy black clouds stretched across the sky and it began to rain. A terrible darkness overtook the whole house. My mother had already been pacing around the house for hours. She hadn't slept the whole night, couldn't get a wink of sleep. A mysterious anxiety didn't let her relax. Although she was eventually expecting a child, it was far too early according to her reckoning. "*Could it come now?*" she thought to herself. "No, there haven't been any *simonim*!"[6]

She paces through all of the rooms, she looks at her little ones: Two girls - Reyzele[7] and Sorkele[8] are sleeping, their beds pushed together. Not far from them sleeps her little boy Yankele.[9] She takes them all in with her loving gaze, and her lips whisper delicately "My dear children." She covers each one separately and quietly leaves the room. She has much work ahead of her today. She has one week until

---

[6]   Signs or indicators.
[7]   This is a Yiddish nickname for Helen's sister Roza.
[8]   This is a Yiddish nickname for Helen's sister Sara.
[9]   This is a Yiddish nickname for Helen's brother Kuba.

Pesach.[10] So much housework this time of year! Washing, scouring, scrubbing . . . and her husband must open the store. Many customers come in to the store, where the shelves are drooping from the weight of the varied merchandise: tapestries, fabrics, boots, toys, and many other things.

Every fancy lady comes all the way here to shop. My mother is well loved. She is always polite, gets along with everyone, and always helps customers find what they need. When my father is in the store (and he is, of course, a great salesman), they always ask about my mother. And now, my mother is wandering and cannot find rest. Something bothers her about this weather, the darkness, the covered sun and the rain. She is uneasy to the bone. Everyone is sleeping soundly, while she stays awake. She sits by the window, opens it, and looks into the street. Today is the 1st of April. Everything is in bloom. From the distance, the fresh spring smell is wafting from mountains and orchards, from fields and forests. Everything in nature is young and pretty. Everything smells and sings spring songs. But why is my mother so lonely? All of a sudden, she feels a sharp pain, something inside of her is moving so powerfully, and her pain increases. Though it hurts her, she wants terribly just to fall asleep. She lets her head fall and she dozes off.

"Rochele, why are you sitting like this, my child?" She hears her mother's voice and feels her warm hands on her shoulder. Go, lie down in bed." "Mother," she answers, "I am in so much pain. I don't know why . . ." Her mother embraces her with her warm stare. She understands everything. My mother had already borne three children, but she still doesn't realize that she is nearing the birth of her fourth. And her mother, my grandmother Sheyndl, literally takes her into her hands and lays her down in bed. She immediately runs out to find a midwife. My mother is heaving and contorting herself because of the pain. She bites her lips, so that her mother shouldn't hear her suffering. Nevertheless, a shrill cry bursts out of her. Grandma runs quickly into the kitchen. She bursts into tears. Her lips, white from fear, whisper a prayer: "*Gotenyu!*[11] Help my child come through in

---

10 Hebrew for the Passover holiday that takes place in the beginning of spring.

11 "My God!" This is a Yiddish expression used as a personal supplication to God.

peace. I beg you father in heaven, make it quick! Don't let my child suffer!" And as she whispers, she hears a voice: "*Mazel Tov, Mazel Tov!*[12] Another daughter!"

My grandma faints from joy, because God granted her request. Everything went so quickly and so smoothly. My grandmother was comforted and she ran to her child. She takes her into her arms and mother and daughter remain attached to one another. Large tears of joy pour from their eyes. We got it over with. "Praised are you, father in heaven!" The first question my mother asked was: "Mother, is it at least a pretty girl? Oy, another girl, the third one already, *kenehora*!"[13] Grandma quickly shuts her mouth: "My child, don't speak like that. A child is a child. You will definitely have a lot of *nachas*,[14] you'll see." My mother put her trust in Grandma's words, and drained from that sleepless night and from all of her pains, she quickly falls into a deep sleep.

And so, on April 1, I came into the world . . .

I was born right at the time when everything was coming to life. All of nature had bloomed and grown wild. The forests broke into song with their birds, who had returned from the warm lands where they find a temporary home while it is winter for us. At this time, everyone was preparing for *Pesach*, the beautiful spring holiday. Every house came to life. Everything was taken outside of the houses in order to lime-wash it and clean out the winter dust. The double windows, which kept everyone warm during the winter, were taken down, the ash of the stove cleaned out, every piece of dirt cast away. The houses were decked in beautiful white curtains, with new sheets on the beds, with various other things, in order to make everything look fresh and pretty.

We always joked that *Pesach* is really for the slobs; the one time of year when they clean out the crusted filth from their houses. And my mother had to choose *davka*[15] this time to give birth! She cannot

---

[12] Congratulations!

[13] This is a Yiddish expression, which means "Against the Evil Eye." It is said after praising or saying something good about someone lest the Evil Eye make a move and thwart the praise.

[14] Pride.

[15] Specifically.

relax. "What will be done?" "Who will do all of this work?" My father is also not happy. He is on his feet since the early morning. The store is open and the customers are pouring in because everyone wants to do their shopping as early as possible. All are in a rush. It's a market day and it's just before *Yontif*.[16]

All of the peasants from the surrounding villages travel to the market in Kremenitz in their long wagons. The wheels are banging on the brick-paved roads and people are pushing and shouting. Here and there, petty fights break out and the shouts of chickens and geese blend in with the peasant voices that bang and shout, calling customers to their wares. Everything you could ever want can be found at the market. The Christians are also celebrating their *Pascha* (Easter), and there is a holiday spirit everywhere. When the peasants are paid for their merchandise, they go into the town and fill up the stores, buying various things. My father is very busy. The day is already half-over and he hasn't had a chance to eat anything. The *goyim*[17] push themselves in *davka* when the stores are full of people, a great opportunity for shoplifting. Indeed, it wasn't uncommon for my father to notice as he closes the store at night, that he is missing a piece of fabric, a small dress and other things.

My father is also a clockmaker. People come from all over to have him fix a single clock, install one small pane or a spring. Sometimes, however, he hits the jackpot; someone comes in selling a piece of gold, which he can resell for a hefty sum.

When my mother is around, all holes get patched up. She is savvy in business and a golden homemaker. Her hands don't get so much as a moment's rest, they are moving and working so fast. One can see her serving the customers, with her signature calm voice speaking to the aristocrats, telling them "*Eto vas podkhoyet.*"[18] They always buy what she has chosen for them.

In the days of Tsar Nikolai, there was a military outpost in Kremenitz. Of course, many officers lived there with their wives. And

---

16 The Yiddish way of referring to certain Jewish holidays.
17 The Yiddish way of referring to gentiles.
18 Russian meaning "This fits you perfectly."

Kremenitz lived off of these aristocrats. Everyone had *parnasah*[19] and, in later years, people frequently harked back to the good old days. My father used to bring it up frequently, licking his lips when he said, "Oh, how good it was under Mikolka,[20] we made a good living from the Russians. Those days will never come back!"

My mother used to sew new clothes for the officers' wives. They used to show them off at the grandest balls. Often, when everyone was asleep late at night, my mother used to sit at her machine. Overnight, new clothing, dresses and peasant aprons were created. She was full of young energy. All were in awe of her, of how much love and talent she put into her work. She would start with her pretty white hands to sew an image of landscapes. The flowers and trees came alive with their natural colors. When you approached them, they would start to give off their natural scent. And here is a second picture: a windmill! When you look into it, you feel like a wind will blow and it will begin to spin. Her lovely artistic hands endured everything just to bring this out.

The house was in bloom. In every corner was a fresh cleanliness. It so sparkled and shone, that you could see your own reflection. And her kids! Here they are, the three well-raised little ones, two girls; the elder Reyzele with black hair, and the younger Sorke, with cherry-black eyes and blond hair. Everyone wondered about the hair: "What's the idea, Rochele? How did you get a blond girl? Not her mother, nor her father, nor even her grandparents have blond hair." My mother smiled, but these comments really bothered her ("such rubbish!"), but what could she do? Nevertheless, this did not diminish her love by one bit. But more than all the others, her love was concentrated on her only son. Yankele, my brother, was chubby with black eyes and with long, white hair, which eventually changed color. He really was a sweet child, and my mother reserved a special love for her "lovely." All of the kids were always well-dressed. The white knitted dresses and blouses brought even more charm to their bright, cheery faces. They stood out, and everyone used to ask: "Who are these kids?" "Those are Rochele and Boruch's kids," people answered. And all thanks to my mother.

---

[19] The Hebrew word for sustenance, but usually used in the context of having a job.

[20] The nickname for Tsar Nikolai.

When my two sisters were in their cribs, my mother used to rock them with one foot and, with the second, she spun the wheel of the sewing-machine. She was never tired, always full of energy and love, like a holy mother.

Sheyndl, my maternal grandmother, had been living with us for a long time. My mother was her only daughter. She had an older son, Hersh, living in Warsaw, and a son from her second marriage, Leybush. My grandmother was a tall, classy woman with a beautiful elegant face that shone with two gorgeous, black and wise eyes. Her long black hair was always covered with a white *tichl*.[21] Those who knew her always said that she was stunning in her youth; this was still visible in the lines of her face. She also was blessed with other positive characteristics: her gentle nature, her wisdom, and her positive outlook on life. I can still see her now, her face and her pretty white hands, how they tirelessly worked. I remember her every movement. Her heartfelt love to all of us kids is deeply impressed into my memory; those to whom one is connected with such a powerful, loving bond are not easily forgotten. I also remember her tormented face, her eyes soaked with pain and suffering. Truthfully, she was miserable.

With her first husband (my mother's father), she lived a happy life, but this joy was short-lived. On a business trip in Besarabia,[22] my grandfather suddenly died of a heart attack at 34 years of age. The bitter news reached my grandmother like thunder from a clear sky. She wept day and night, embittered, broken, with two still-young children. Until her final days, she mourned her beloved, who perished abroad, without friends or relatives to look upon with his final gaze.

My grandmother suffered silently, bottled everything up inside, and her heart grew weaker and weaker. Everything stopped inside of her, even her will to live. "But the children," she thought. "What did they do wrong?" "Do I have the right to leave them behind?" And she roused herself from her depression, picked herself up and took up the struggle of life again.

---

21 A scarf that was worn over the head to cover a woman's hair.
22 This is the historical term for the geographic region in Eastern Europe between the Dniester and Prut Rivers.

She sewed clothing for strangers, patched socks, and didn't neglect her children. And the small cottage in which she lived shone with cleanliness. Her older son grew to be an outstanding child, with great talents. There was no one in his school that could study and advance from one class to the other with such phenomenal grades in every subject. Hersh Koltun was the name of the boy, with whom all of Kremenitz prided itself. He was invited to wealthy homes to help the rich kids with their studies, and he earned a nice living. He gave every penny to his mother, which was tremendously helpful.[23]

---

[23] At this point in her journal, my grandmother abruptly stops writing. It is my assumption that she intended to continue writing at a later date but never had the opportunity.

Rochele with her daughter Helen

| Chapter Three |

THE MATURA

Kremenitz 1927

The Matura is an interesting autobiographical account of my grandmother's experience prior to taking her entrance exam into high school. This section was written by my grandmother as a flashback to her experience during this memorable time.

Growing up, we were always aware of our grandmother's brilliance, amazed that she was fluent in so many languages: English, Hebrew, Yiddish, Russian, Ukrainian, Polish, Latin, German, and a working knowledge of French. My grandmother possessed an impressive diligence when learning new information. I found a number of notebooks and scrap papers that she saved, stored away in closets or drawers, on which she would practice her English. There were soliloquies, paragraphs from random books, even quotes from famous individuals. She was always challenging herself, determined to advance her opportunities in society.

Of note is the fact that in this selection, she refers to herself with a pseudonym, Chavtzi Rubin. This is a wonderful example of the humility that she displayed both in her everyday life as well as in her writings, never wanting to draw attention to or boast about her intellectual prowess.

Helen as a carefree young girl

Helen enjoying nature as a young girl

Students in the 8th grade of *gymnasium*[24] have already been preparing for the *matura* for a long time. This is the last test of high school before one can begin to study in university. Everyone studied feverishly. The houses were littered with various books and notebooks and piles of notes, and many other necessary things for the exam. It was not easy. The facts would get mixed up in your head. How will I remember all of this? How can I gather so much information in such a small head? Math with its various rules, physics, history, geography, Polish literature, Latin, French, chemistry, anatomy, and much, much more . . . memorizing historical dates and skimming books. Who can keep track of all of it? Understandably, everyone's heart was filled with dread. One person was weak in math. Another remembered literature well, but was terrified of physics. So we all crammed day and night, shutting out the rest of the world.

The exam takes place right at the end of spring and the beginning of summer, when nature is so beautiful and rich and every detail tries to distract us, calls us forth: "Come play with me. Enjoy my richness! I will reward you with pretty flowers and sweet music from the deep enchanted forest! Come, come, make haste, time is ticking!" But how can one go out into nature when the books summon us with a different voice? "Stay here, study well, a little bit more and you will laugh at the rest of the world. In the meantime, be strong and resist the beautiful temptation of nature. Surely you don't want to let a whole year go to waste, an entire year! You know how much this will hurt your parents? And you yourself? You will be humiliated when you fail the exam! How will you look the sun in the eyes? How will you face the deep fragrant forest if you do not accomplish this? No, don't let yourself be deceived! Be consistent! It won't be long!" So I keep studying. I go over dozens of times the mathematical formulae, the trigonometry and logarithms. The Latin words, with their complicated grammar. Remember everything. Everything.

It is such a *rachmones*[25] to look into the pale faces of the students as the exam looms closer. Oh, matura, matura! Are you really so valuable? Are you worth all of these precious moments of life that we give up for you?

---

[24] The Polish word for high school.

[25] Pity.

The time of the exam is coming closer and closer. Just one week left . . . only three days . . . one day . . . tomorrow is judgment day. Every heart is beating fast. Everyone silently whispers, *"Gotenyu[26] help me!"* "Good luck," we wish everyone. All are dressed up *yontifdik[27]* with a forced smile on their faces. The bell rings and so does every heart, with a shudder.

The exam lasts for five days. They ask about everything that was learned over the years. All of the teachers, the principal, and the chairman of the Curatorium were gathered around a long table that was decked out in fluffy green fabric (green = the color of hope), and all pose their questions. You write your answers on a board. All of your mental energy is concentrated on these questions. You want to answer to the best of your ability.

Many of us have been told to leave the room. You can tell from the look on people's faces, who has done well and who has not. People are jealous of one another, but at least it is mostly over. In the last row remained one person: the quiet and pale girl, Chavtzi Rubin. Why was she so deathly pale? Why was she so much more afraid than the others? Wasn't she prepared? Was she missing something? Chavtzi was renowned and loved by all of the teachers. Everyone knew about her shining talents in every field. Before she was called back into the exam room, she paced nervously in the corridor. Her lips were pale.

The principal noticed her. "Chavtzi," he called to her, "What's going on? You are so pale! Don't worry, you know how learned you are. This exam is a joke for you. Go in boldly, don't be scared. Anyway, based on our calculations, you will definitely pass, no matter what happens." The director's words calmed Chavtzi down. Everyone knows that Chavtzi is the best student of all and that she passes from one class to another with flying colors. Her parents are poor. Though they struggle hard for a piece of bread, their daughter is the first in class and the most diligent student. Always dressed pristinely in her old dresses, always cheerful with her beautiful shining eyes, in which knowledge and wisdom reside. Who knows how often she is so hungry that her head spins and she cannot learn . . . but she is always the first.

---

[26] "My God!" This is a Yiddish expression used as a personal supplication to God.

[27] Appropriate for the holidays.

When her parents come to ask about their daughter, they always receive the same report: Your child is the crown of our school. She is an outstanding student, and you should be proud of her. Naturally, her parents are happy with this answer, but they do not dwell on it; their heads are filled with only one idea: Where do we find *parnasah*?[28]

Chavtzi was skinny because she didn't have enough food, but she was pretty and smart, and because of her talents, she learned as well as only rich kids can. She didn't pay for school. She earned some money on the side teaching students from younger grades and all that she earned, she gave to her parents, and so became even more beloved by everyone.

Now she is finishing gymnasium. Today she receives her matura and she will be eligible to pursue higher learning. She is afraid. She might forget something when they ask her the final few questions. How would she face the world?

Her whole life, she did not let anyone take her glory. She was always the winner, always first place. She was, perhaps, too proud of this fact. Whenever a competitor threatened her, she jealously bit her lips and decided not to allow anyone to be better than she was.

She was asked several questions. Chavtzi answered calmly and boldly. Her answers projected intelligence and knowledge in every instance. They accepted her answers enthusiastically. Words like pearls were pouring from her lips. They didn't let her finish. The chairman interrupted her, "Enough Ms. Rubin. Your answers reveal a deep learning. It has been a long time since I have heard anything like it." Pointing to the matura exams, he continued: "You have passed with excellent grades and in addition, yours is the best matura in the whole class." Everyone shakes her hand, all celebrate with her. Chavtzi is on everyone's lips, people speak about her excitedly. At the door, the parents of the rich students stand. They greet their children with great pomp. Whether they aced the test or just barely passed, everyone was relieved just to get the piece of paper, the *matura*. No one is waiting for Chavtzi. Her father is *nebekh*[29] working hard, and her mother is sick. Chavtzi runs quickly to her parents to tell them the good news. All of the parents look at her. How happy they would be to have such

---

[28] The Hebrew word for sustenance, but usually used in the context of having a job.

[29] Unfortunately or unfortunate soul.

a good kid! They would buy her such nice presents and the whole world would cheer. Chavtzi runs very fast. Her "friends" are keeping a distance from her, watching her with envy and speaking loudly so that she will hear: "She probably failed the exam. What, she thinks she will always be such a hotshot?" They don't know how joyous this day is for Chavtzi, she is the first and the best. She has accomplished her goal. She is undefeated.

The sun is shining for her much brighter than usual. Today the birds are singing their songs of praise just for her. She goes to relax in the deep enchanted forest. She will lie on the grass and inhale the aromas of various flowers that grow all over. She will let her fantasies and dreams of the great world overtake her. She will relive the precious moments of this day, the wonderful words of the chairman, the congratulations that the teachers and the principal gave her. She must no longer sit up late in the night and bury herself in books. She will rest and enjoy the rich and delightful summer.

The world is hers now . . . .

Helen before outbreak of World War Two

| Chapter Four |

WHITE ANGELS

Krakow 1939

In the nursing school they called us **"White Angels."** An angel in our imagination is something divine and supreme; something that does not belong to the earth. Almost everyone is convinced that in heaven there are living angels, noble beings with wings on their shoulders willing at any time to perform the functions God designed for them. Very often these God-like beings are sent down to earth for the sake of bringing relief to people experiencing either physical or mental suffering. It seems very likely that nurses in white uniforms, although without wings, are sent from God to do their duty put upon them from the day of their birth.

A nurse is then the spirit which is always helpful, always bringing aid and relief to those who demand it the most. What could be more meaningful and noble than to give love, understanding and sympathy to human suffering, and at the same time, to be able to help cure their pain?

Each one of us had in our lives the experience to be in a hospital for one reason or another. Sometimes, it was with high temperature, seeking help and relief from the pain. Suddenly we start to get well because we feel a touch of a warm, soft nurse's hand. It is like a mother's or an angel's touch which cures instantly.

I remember when I was six years old, I entered the hospital for a minor operation. I saw nurses for the first time in my life and I fell

in love with them. That was when I made up my mind to become a nurse.

Sometimes an insignificant event in our youngest years puts the mark on our future life. We decide what we want to become in the future and as we grow older, we try to realize our dreams, our desires and ideas. With longing I had waited for my graduation from high school to have the opportunity to make my dream come true choosing my career of nursing. Many times while dreaming I had seen myself in a nurse's uniform and like an angel flying on wings to the suffering to comfort them and bring them hope and happiness.

Relatives and friends discouraged me from becoming a nurse. They tried to convince me that nursing was the most difficult profession in the world and I shouldn't sacrifice my life for the hardest. But nobody in the world could change my mind. My decision had been made since my childhood. There was only one person, whom I never have forgotten - my dear mother - who understood me then the most. Her words of encouragement made me the happiest person in the world.

The time approached for my departure from home to another city. I was young and ambitious, full of strength and persistence. The big world greeted me with open arms. At that time I loved the world and every person and creature living in it. Life was beautiful and full of colors and songs. I expected to work hard for three years and I was ready for it. I wasn't a child anymore. I moved far from home to build my own future and the next chapter of my life. There was something in me that resembled Florence Nightingale, a reformer of nurses who was trained to challenge every difficult situation with love and patience.

I began a new life. From the moment I put on my nurse's uniform, I decided to put all my focus on my duties and I deserved to be called a nurse. I lived in the hospital where I studied and worked. A hospital is a world of its own. People staying in the hospital are different from others. They are unhappy and often times don't have any hope to become well again. We nurses have to help them in many ways, sacrificing sometimes, even our personal life.

The beginning was the hardest until I got acquainted with the work and the environment. But through it all, I was very homesick. I missed my beloved family, my school friends, and the town which

was beautiful in every season of the year. It was there where I spent the first years of my life in happiness, with joy and dreams.

However, I loved the great work I was doing and chose to stay with the sick people. I saw in their eyes and heard in their voices the great need for help. "Come, come white angel. Don't leave us, we need you." I realized then that I reached the highest point in my life and found the secret to my happiness - helping others.

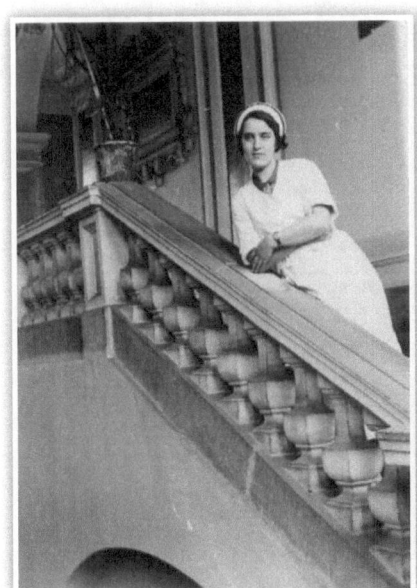

Helen as a nurse in Krakow

PRESIDENT 4-1300

JACOB DAMASZEK, M. D.
1347 EASTERN PARKWAY
BROOKLYN 33, N. Y.

September 10, 1954

To Whom It May Concern: Re: Mrs. Helena Gun Weinberg

During the period between 1935 and 1937, while I was employed as a physician at the Jewish Hospital in Krakov, Poland, I met Mrs. Helena Gun Weinberg who was at that time employed as a graduate nurse in the department of internal medicine, where I was at that time employed.

Mrs. Weinberg had completed a 3 year course in nursing at that hospital and passed her examination before a government commission as a graduate nurse.

This qualified her to work in her profession in any hospital in Poland.

It is my understanding that Mrs. Weinberg has been employed in surgery, internal medicine, the children's ward and the clinic of the hospital.

I am sorry that I am unable to offer any additional information regarding Mrs. Weinberg subsequent to that period as I left the hospital in 1938.

Mrs. Weinberg impressed me with her conscienciousness, skill, efficiency, pleasing manner and high moral character.

I am pleased to be able to say a few words in her behalf.

Very truly yours,

J. Damaszek M.D.

Helen, fourth from left, in nursing school in Krakow

PRESIDIUM
OF THE NATIONAL COUNCIL
IN CRACOV
DEPARTMENT OF HEALTH
L.Zd.V1_11/25/57

Cracov, March 1, 1957.

CERTIFICATE

I,Michalina Wilczynska,former state instructor of nursing in Cracov, hereby certify that Miss Jenta (Helen) Gun passed in 1938,a nursing examination before a Government Examination Comission of the then State Department of Health in Cracov.

She finished the course,passed the state board examination,and received her diploma.That diploma authorized her to performe as a professional nurse in the entire state of Poland.

All the documents that could affirm this declaration were destroyed during the occupation,and officialy besides my declaration as a member of the Board of Examination,and a nursing instructor we are unable to offer anything further.

Michalina Wilczynska
Nursing Instructor

Presidium Of The National Council
Department Of Health in Cracov,confirm Miss M.Wilczynska's authenttic signature,and certify that Miss M WILCZYNSKA performed the performed the function of state nursing instructor from 1933 to 1939

Department of Staff
Janina Tarko
Chief of the Department.

Letter certifying Helen's nursing degree

Chapter Five

WORLD WAR TWO

Poland 1940

In order to fully appreciate the following segment, it is necessary to understand the absolute horror that was accompanied by experiences of incarceration, beatings, executions, starvation and cruelties. While it is true that the Nazis were barbaric, the Russians under Stalin were not that different. The Nazis were looking to exterminate Jews whereas Stalin was looking to kill anyone who opposed the Soviet Union. There was much overlap in the techniques and methods used in various labor camps. Most notably were the sheer brutality and inhumane circumstances brought upon millions of innocent people, Jews a large segment amongst them.

When the reality of Russian concentration camps or labor camps first emerged, they simply served as isolating prisons with minimal use of forced labor. The work was very difficult and often senseless. The number of laborers continued to grow while the prisoners died from malnutrition and heavy work that exceeded their strength. This is the reality to which my grandmother was introduced. A reality of senseless hardship, meaningless interrogations and, worst of all, a systematic deprivation of all things human . . .

Life became harder with every passing day. Food was difficult to get and I began to feel pangs of hunger. It is so hard to express how homesick I was. Thoughts and concerns for my dear family consumed me. It felt like they were thousands of miles away:

I still long for you my beloved town Kremenitz.
In my dreams you are with me,
in my dreams you are without bounds.
You occupy the majority of my memories,
for how can I forget you for even a minute,
because my heart pounds so hard for you,
and longs for every pebble and wooden beam in the house,
in which I saw the world for the first time.
Where are you now my town, my home?
Why was your end so horrible?
I seek you all my loved ones,
I lived with you my whole life.
What is this all worth without you,
all my struggles and aspirations?
I can't find peace anymore,
my happiness I can't reach.
Until the word is no longer in my thoughts,
I will constantly remember it.
Just like in a rich beautiful mild May,
so too I will be renewed.
My dear town with small streets, bedecked in green and blooming trees.
To you, my pristine town,
I will erect a monument,
forever to be remembered.
I gnaw for you, I long for you.
Forever I will experience the sounds of my city's songs.

Poland was divided in two parts: One belonged to the occupation of the Germans while the other part, to the Soviet Union. A border was built and established through the River San. That was the border that set me apart from my family. I was on the German side, they on the Russian side. My problem was crossing this "artificial" border and the river. I had the courage to go through many difficulties, which

threatened my life by coming close to that border. It was the end of the month of October. On both sides of the river stood armed guards watching, uninterrupted day and night, in order to prevent people from crossing the border. Some of my friends were good swimmers and decided to swim across that river in the darkness of the night. I had to refrain from doing that since I couldn't swim and decided to wait until the river was frozen to make my way across it.

The waiting period was extremely hard. Every day new orders by the Nazis against the Jews emerged. Jews were forced to wear armbands with the Star of David and they were sent to labor camps. They were punished for every little thing that they felt was wrong - even punished with death. We were treated worse than animals and of course we weren't permitted even to complain. We were full-fledged slaves bitten and tormented. They tried to make us forget that we were human beings. And that was just the beginning of the horrible days awaiting us from those barbarians of the twentieth century - the Germans.

News came that ghettos and isolation - concentration - camps, were being built in order to liquidate the Jews. In the beginning we tried to ignore the news and lived with hope that the war would soon be over with the defeat of the Germans and we would return to normal life. But time didn't show any signs of a quick end to the war. Our suffering became more severe and we started to believe the horrible news in earnest.

Chapter Six

THE ESCAPE

December, 1940

December arrived with its cold and freezing weather, and was for me the time to get away from the waiting dark days of the future. I couldn't think of anything else but of my escape. Together with a few of my friends, we left Krakow and, after many hard days of struggling, we were ready to cross the frozen River San.

The night was dark. A cold wind blew from the river and the surrounding hills. It was gusting around us and we didn't see a single living creature. Everything seemed to be working out for us but it was dangerous at the same time because any wrong move could be fatal. We didn't see any German guards and we didn't even think of the Russians. The hope that we would soon be on the other side and closer to a reunion with our families gave us much courage.

We crossed the German part of the border and almost reached the other side when suddenly we heard shots and screams. We stopped with our hands up as ordered. I felt as if the blood froze in my veins when I saw so many Russian soldiers armed with guns and rifles pointed directly at us. We were ordered to lie down with our faces in the snow while they searched our baggage for arms and explosives.

It's hard to give an exact account of how long we were laying in the snow. It seemed to me forever. I was all frozen and stiff from the

cold and couldn't move a finger. Maybe this is the end, I thought, while I lost all my hope to be home again.

The night ended when big trucks arrived to rush us to a nearby prison. We were guarded as though we were bad criminals. That same night, and for many hours, I was questioned and accused of crossing the border in order to spy for the Germans. They didn't believe my answers that the only crime I committed was saving my life by escaping from the Germans in order to be together with my family, which was on the Russian side.

The next day I was transferred to another prison and was kept there as a real prisoner with continuous questioning and the same accusations against me over and over. After a week in prison, many of us including me, were put in cattle wagons with small grated windows and heavily guarded and sent to the unknown. Nobody knew where we were headed or for how long. When we asked them if we would remain in a prison (at that time we were unaware of their prisons and terrible concentration camps), they assured us that the Soviet Union doesn't have any prisons like the capitalistic countries, and that we will be so happy to be in a great country to work and to build a happy life for ourselves.

In front of the wagon in which I was locked, a man was passing the tracks and with tears in his eyes told us that the Russians are taking us not to a paradise but to prisons and labor camps for a long period of time. Once we are in their hands it will be impossible to get our freedom. It is easy therefore to imagine my feelings at that time. "Will I survive all this?" I thought. "Is it worth fighting for this miserable life of ours?" "What can we then expect from the future?" Everything around me was dark and hopeless. I prayed to God to give me strength to live through this hell.

It was midnight when the convoy of many wagons with many "terrible" criminals in them started moving far away from the country where I was born and from my home and dear family. We were rushed because the Russians perform their work at night and as we learned, everything of most importance is done only in the night hours when the world is covered with darkness and when nobody could discover their "devilish work".

For eight days we were traveling, stopping for a while to pick up some more victims. Food consisted of bread and water (sometimes hot

water and salty fish). The wagon was small and 25 people in it made life just horrible. However, all those inconveniences with hunger and living in dirt didn't make me as sad as the feelings of being a prisoner. I lost my freedom and without the freedom I loved so much, I felt lost in the world with no hope of surviving.

Finally, we approached Odessa, the beautiful city by the shores of the Black Sea. Through the little window we felt the pleasant breeze coming from the sea. I even smelled the salty water from the dancing waves. I thought how wonderful it would be to find myself in that magic place, forget all the burdens of life only to enjoy the beauty of nature. But reality was very cruel.

We had barely left the cold and dirty, weeks-long train ride that took us from Lemberg through the entire Russian empire to Novo-Sibersk, and our troubles started anew. The clattering of the train, the cries of children and women, and the sighing of the elderly rang so sadly in our ears, as if a painful shriek had burst forth from our hearts. Where are we? What will they do with us?

All of a sudden, a huge forest emerged in front of us. It jutted in all directions, getting deeper and thicker, with wide, tall trees and grasses. Not a trace of human life. Here we had to build a new city for Stalin, for the almighty Russian flag. And here we had to remain *"na vsiegda,"* forever, as our train conductor told us after leaving us here.

Every one of us felt a deep sadness in our hearts. Our limbs seemed to die within us. We were ordered to get out of the train and slept in front of a large building. It was midnight again. On the top of the building a red star was shining - a symbol of happiness, a circle with a hammer - another symbol of work - and the key to that "happy life" in the Soviet Union.

The doors were wide open for us and step by step swallowed us inside the dark, cold, horrible and never forgotten walls of a Russian prison. I was placed in a small cell with nine other women, a cell too small for three people. As the heavy doors closed, the words of the Russian soldiers echoed in my ears, "The Soviet Union doesn't possess any prisons."

I looked around and had the feeling that those four walls must be soaked through and through with human tears and blood and suffering. I had the desire to scream with all the strength that was left in me and to cry out from all my pain from the wound so deep inside

me, but I wasn't able to scream or cry or even say a word. And so began the next chapter of my life. I could have never imagined this life, not even in my worst nightmares.

All the people brought from Poland were placed on the second floor, isolated from the other Russian prisoners. Knowing some Russian I was able to communicate with them and when I asked them why they brought me here, their answer was to educate us in order to be fit for their socialistic country and their way of life. Since Poland didn't exist anymore, the Soviet Union would have become my country. "But why this way - through imprisonment?" I asked in wonderment. Their answer was that there had to be a punishment for a "big crime" of illegally crossing the border. I believed that once I could convince them of my innocence, I would be free to enjoy the "beautiful life" in the "heaven" of the Soviet Union. There wasn't any choice but to wait and see how much truth was in their words of assurance.

The food was very poor - a piece of bread (400 grams) and a watery soup twice a day. No vegetables of any kind. Even an onion would have been a luxury! As we were so far from home there was no question of receiving anything from the outside. We slept on the naked cement floor with our blankets to cover ourselves, and lack of fresh air made our suffering more severe. But all that was nothing in comparison with those nightly interrogations.

After a terrible day of hunger and exhaustion, I waited impatiently for the night in order to have a few hours of sleep so as to forget all the burdens I endured. They took me out from the cell to the office of the investigator and again asked me the same questions, "Why did I cross the border and what mission was I to fulfill for the Germans?" My answer time and again was that I was a Jew escaping from the Germans in order to save my life but this didn't satisfy the barbarian at all. He wanted the truth (even according to their slogans that for the truth you are punished). He wanted me to confess to something I didn't do. How could I confess to a crime I didn't commit? I cried with tears of blood and pain. He didn't believe me because Moscow doesn't believe in tears. This attention was to prove a fantastic case of espionage where I as the victim could be sent to prison or to concentration camps for many years or even receive the death penalty.

Many times after unsuccessful interrogations I was locked in an isolation cell for five days on bread and water only. When that still didn't get them the answers they wanted, I was beaten with a stick over my head that made me faint. Unconscious and covered with blood I was put back to my cell. But after regaining my consciousness, I had to return to the old routine of those nightly questionings which became a terrible nightmare and drove many people insane and even to commit suicide. I could often hear cries and screams from other cells which echoed with horror. The outside world didn't know what was going on inside those walls. They wouldn't have believed it anyway even if someone had pictured it for them.

The war continued to destroy more human lives. We didn't know what was going on outside. From time to time, some good Soviets gave us scraps of news. We painfully learned how the Germans occupied one country after another and we knew what this meant for their population, especially for the Jews. I was sick and hungry and very concerned about my dear ones. There seemed no hope that I would ever come out alive as a free person. It was like the devil himself was performing his art, causing destruction and the loss of innocent lives. What was the purpose?

While walking in the prison yard I could see the horrid condition of the other prisoners and my heart hurt me looking at them, especially when I saw so many young children who spent their childhood in a prison cell for a non-existent crime.

Days and weeks had passed with no changes in our lives. When summer arrived with the hot weather, we suffered very much from the heat and I, as many others, became ill with dysentery. This prevented our investigators from questioning us on their nightly routine, out of fear of catching it themselves. Then came a time when it was just impossible to continue the prison routine and we started demanding that they should send us to the labor camps where the conditions would be a little improved, but most of all we were looking forward to fresh air. We organized a hunger strike, knowing full well that strikes are forbidden in Russia, but we had to do it. We considered the worst that could happen to us - but nothing could be worse than what we were living. They had to do something not to starve us to death.

Without a trial everybody received his or her sentence of three to five years in a labor camp. I received five years in a labor camp. Five

years of my life were taken away from me for illegally crossing the border and I was sent to a place not far from Arkhangelsk which lies on the banks of the Northern Dvina River and the White Sea in the north of Russia.

After spending 18 months in a prison, in an endless nightmare of hunger and sickness, tortures, pain and suffering where I almost lost the image of being a human being, I began a life of a slave. I had to work in the fields planting vegetables, mostly potatoes, and also in the forests together with men chopping trees which were used for building barracks for prisoners and as wood for fuel. Winter lasts almost 10 months of the year there and it is extremely cold. Food was not much better than in prison, but we had fresh air and moved more freely even though we were still under the watchful eyes of armed guards.

I had the opportunity to speak to Russians who were deported there for 10 to 15 years. They were very nice and intelligent but at the same time very unhappy and hopeless of regaining their freedom. They were also in those camps for crimes they didn't commit. Accused of being an enemy to their country, they were tortured until they confessed to everything.

There were many prison and concentration camps all over the country filled with millions of innocent people, suffering and hopeless for a better future. Even one single word said against the Russian ideology resulted in years of imprisonment or even worse - concentration camps. People lived afraid of their own shadows.

In June of 1941, the German-Russian war began. Just prior to this they were friends bound by pacts and agreements and suddenly they were enemies. Two barbarian countries stood against each other in a duel to conquer and enslave the free world.

After the United States came to help Russia in her struggles to defeat the Germans, an agreement between the two freed the Polish citizens from prison and the concentration camps. So freedom came for me unexpectedly but without much joy and happiness. What would freedom look like on the Russian territory?

My Russian friends, with whom I spent a short time of only six months, wished me luck on my journey to freedom but at the same time were jealous of me. I saw it in their eyes when they said their last

goodbye to me. I cried and was sorry for them for not being able to help them. I just promised them to bring out to the open the truth about their tragedy and suffering.

This time the doors to freedom were wide open for me. Freedom! Freedom! A great and sweet sound, but when I looked behind me I was sad. I once again saw the red shining star on the top of the camp. I hallucinated seeing blood running from that star. All around - blood and tears coming from years of pain and suffering.

I was a prisoner no more. I was a free person yet I was alone in this gigantic and strange country. My life was still very difficult and filled with many struggles of hunger and sickness. With many others, I tried to reach a place with a warm climate. I finally came to Samarkand, a city in Middle Asia. I was happy to reunite with a man who also came out of a labor camp somewhere in Siberia. We were married on January 1, 1942.

Together we began a new life of struggles and hardships in the hope that someday we would live to see a better future. By working together, we could more or less support ourselves. But then I was stricken with malaria and typhoid fever. I was so ill; there was no hope of recovering.

Chapter Seven

BARUCH CHAIM

Samarkand 1944

After a long period of time, miraculously, I recovered from those horrible diseases but I wasn't able to work anymore and I had to depend solely on my husband's support. He had to share his ration of bread with me, which only a working person received by showing his working card.[30]

I was weak and always hungry, nervous and hysterical especially when I found out I was pregnant. But on November 16, 1944, I gave birth to a beautiful baby boy[31] and I was very happy and tried to forget all the burdens around me.[32] I lived and fought all the difficulties of life only for that child.

The war was coming to an end. The Germans suffered defeat on every front and had to retreat. May 8, 1945 marked the day the

---

[30]   They were reduced to scrounging through garbage cans to eat discarded potato peels so as to supplement their meager diet.

[31]   My grandmother's first son, my father, was given the name Baruch Chaim in memory of her father. In Hebrew the combined name means "Blessed is Life" - a true testimony to survival.

[32]   On the night that my grandmother went into labor, my grandfather and cousin Yosef Zaltz walked with her through the snow and freezing cold to the hospital where she gave birth.

war was over. People were happy, of course, and there was joy in the street. Everyone including myself wanted to see the end of the war. But joy disappeared when I learned that almost all the members of my husband's and my family were killed and that six million Jews were killed or burned alive simply because they were Jews. I lost my desire to continue my life, but I thought about my child and all my promises to raise him. There was no other choice but to put forth all my efforts and courage and go on with life.

By the end of 1945, Polish citizens were permitted to return to Poland. The Russians supplied us with the cattle wagons in which they brought us to the Soviet Union and some food. This time, we were free people and there were no more armed guards.

After traveling for two weeks we finally came back to Poland.[33] It was there that I saw destruction that I couldn't have imagined. I saw the remains of the concentration camps of Auschwitz, Treblinka and others - the horrors that the Germans left behind. Shocked from all this and almost broken in pieces, I just couldn't believe it. For the first time, I realized the extent of the greatest tragedy of our times.

I decided to run, to run far away from that hell. I started crossing borders. With my husband and little child in my arms I ran day and night.[34] There wasn't any place for us to live. We became displaced

---

[33] After the war, my grandparents went to Krakow in search of relatives who may have survived. My grandfather found a non-Jewish acquaintance who told him that he was shocked to see he was still alive and then made an anti-Semitic comment, insinuating that he would kill him. My grandparents quickly left Krakow and escaped death yet again.

[34] One of the most heart-wrenching stories I heard was when my grandparents were on the run with my father as a baby. They were traveling and hiding in the forests as they were smuggled through Poland and Czechoslovakia dressed as Greek peasants. They tried to outrun the communists and the anti-Semites who were out in droves killing as many Jews as possible before a martial law came into effect. On the way to Austria, to the allied zone (Ulm was the last stop), my father had an ear infection and was crying and shrieking in pain. He was inconsolable and the Jews with whom they were hiding became nervous. My grandmother had to hold his mouth shut so as to stop him from crying and maintain their safety as well as that of those around them. My father fell unconscious just short of suffocating to death.

people and the world didn't know what to do with us. Even in my mind I was running day and night, an eternity of running away so as not to be caught and imprisoned again. I became paranoid and developed deep feelings of fear. I had nightmares and woke up screaming and crying in the middle of the night. I was very close to having a nervous breakdown.

We arrived in a Displaced Persons camp in Ulm, Germany, where I had better food and life was much easier. Yet still I was nervous and jumpy and somehow afraid that something would happen to me in connection with those experiences from my past. I couldn't enjoy life to its fullest extent. Then, I was given another gift.

| Helen, Baruch Chaim, and Yaakov Weinberg | Yaakov Weinberg and Baruch Chaim |

Baruch Chaim, Age 2

Helen walking next to Yaakov in DP camp
(Helen is carrying Baruch Chaim)

Baruch Chaim on Helen's lap with Yaakov in DP Camp

| Chapter Eight |

AARON ASHER

Ulm 1947

*I*n *July of 1947, with the hope of starting a new life in the Jewish homeland of Palestine, my grandparents tried to board the ship Exodus. In order to travel on the Exodus, every passenger was examined by a doctor to ensure no one was carrying a disease that could spread throughout the ship. Upon examination, the doctor learned that my grandmother was in her ninth month of pregnancy and did not allow her to board.*

The Exodus departed France with a destination of Palestine on July 11, 1947, carrying over 4,000 European immigrants. When the ship neared the coast of Palestine a week later, the British, in an attempt to stem immigration, turned the ship back. In the process, several people were killed or wounded. Although my grandparents desperately wanted to put their horrid experiences of World War Two behind them, and immigrate to the Jewish homeland, they were spared a dangerous voyage on the Exodus. They remained hopeful and had faith in God that their day of freedom would soon come . . .

Helen, Aaron Asher, and
Baruch Chaim

Aaron Asher, Yaakov, and
Baruch Chaim

Helen and Aaron Asher

Aaron Asher Age 1

INTERNATIONAL REFUGEE ORGANIZATION
Area 2, Sub-Area Ulm
HEALTH DIVISION

Tel : 3889   APO 154   US ARMY   1 June 1949

TO WHOM IT MAY CONCERN :

      This is to certify that W E I N B E R G , Helene
is working with the I R O in ULM SEDAN CAMP DISPENSARY
as Chief Nurse since 1 September 1948.

R. LUND-JENSEN
Area Nurse
Sub-Areas Ulm & Schw, Gmuend

A confirmation record of Helen's employment
as Chief Nurse in Ulm DP Camp.

Front cover of working papers and identification

Inner page of working papers

Ausfertigung.

Akten Nr. 4772.

U l m a.D.,

Verhandelt am 10. Mai 1948.

Vor mir, dem

Notar T h ö n y in Ulm a.D.,

erscheint heute, geschäftsfähig und durch

ihre D.P. Karte Nr. 625221 ausgewiesen:

Helena W e i n b e r g geb. Gun, Ehefrau

des Jakob Weinberg, Elektrotechnikers,

zur Zeit im Jro-Lager Sedanstrasse 43

in Ulm a.D.,

und erklärt folgende

eidesstattliche Versicherung:

Ich bin geboren am 1. April 1914 in Krzemieniec (Polen) als

Tochter des Baruch-Chaim Gun, Uhrmachers daselbst und seiner

Ehefrau Rachel geborene Koltun.

Als Zeugen sind miterschienen, geschäftsfähig und durch ihre

D.P. Karten ausgewiesen:

1) Frojm W a j z e r , Tischler, z.Zt. Ulm, Sedanstrasse 43

2) Bernat F e u e r , Kaufmann, z.Zt. Ulm a.D., Sedankaserne,

und erklären:

Wir kennen die Helena Weinberg geborene Gun seit ihrer Jugend,

da wir in der gleichen Stadt wie sie gewohnt haben. Wir kannten

auch ihre Mutter. Wenn wir auch den angegebenen Tag ihrer Geburt

Translated on next page

Negotiated 10:00 A.M. May 1948

Before me today, appears the notary Thony in Ulm. The transactions are through his capabilities, the D.P. Card numbers (of the individuals before us) are #610326 and #625221 that are being reported.

1) Jakob Weinberg an electrician who is currently living on 43 Sedan Street in Ulm.
2) His wife Helen Weinberg born Gun explained the following affidavit:
On January 1, 1942 we were married in Samarkand according to Jewish law. On November 16, 1944 a child was born to us in Samarkand his name - Baruch Chaim Weinberg. The child lives with us.

The witnesses are individuals who appear to have legal capacity and by their D.P. cards shown:

1) Froim Wajzner, carpenter, currently living on 43 Sedan Street Ulm.
2) Bernat Feuer, businessman, currently living in Ulm in the Sedan-Barracks.

Who explain:

We also lived in Krakau and the former residence of the Weinbergs is known to us for many years. The data that we are giving may not be precise in all the details, but in other respects we affirm the correctness of the rest of the details regarding the Weinberg spouses. Once the appearing parties had been instructed on the importance of this affidavit information was given of which some information may still not have been included.

Read, approved and signed	Bernat Feuer
Jakob Weinberg	Notar Thony
Helen Weinberg	Done!
Froim Wajzner	Ulm May 10, 1948

On May 14, 1948, the day before the British Mandate was due to expire, David Ben Gurion declared the establishment of the Jewish State of Israel. There was a sense of communal happiness and elation as the hopes and dreams of the Jewish people came to fruition. During their time in Ulm, my grandparents were active with the Breicha[35] and worked to smuggle Jews to then Palestine. They tried to support Israel in any way that they could. They viewed Israel as the antidote to those who sought to destroy the Jewish people. It was more than just a country, it was the establishment of a place of refuge for all Jews.

From my earliest recollections, my grandparents were always involved in Israel's betterment and growth in some fashion. In addition to generously supporting numerous charities and organizations to the best of their ability, they made sure their home was a shrine to the Jewish homeland. I vividly remember the little knick-knacks and trinkets from Israel that adorned their breakfront. They displayed the memorabilia with a sense of pride. Israel was often a topic of conversation on my visits to my grandparents' home. "What do you think about the situation in Israel?" "Will there ever be peace?" These questions were deep concerns for my grandparents and indicative of a real passion they possessed for the country and its citizens. For my grandparents, the establishment of the State of Israel was an event, which signified that Jews would no longer be without a home.

---

[35] This was an organization which worked to bring European refugees to Palestine.

Children of the DP Camp celebrating Israel Independence Day
(Baruch Chaim bottom row, third from right)

Helen and Yaakov celebrating Israel Independence Day

The following letter, written by my grandmother in her native Polish tongue to her brother Kuba (Yaakov Gun) in Israel, bespeaks the uncertainty that my grandmother faced in advance of leaving Ulm. Was she to move to Israel where there was tremendous destabilization in the young economy, work was scarce and war was imminent? Or were they to immigrate to America where my grandfather's uncle, Hersh Weinberg, would sponsor them to obtain visas? One can sense the frustrating dilemma in my grandmother's words. They were stateless and homeless with two small children. She needed to make a decision that would afford her family safety, security and opportunity . . .

Ulm, 25/1, 49

Moi drodzy i kochani!

Wasz list z 6 i b.r. otrzymaliśmy wczoraj i już Wam odpiszę. Ogromnie Wam dziękuję, że jednak nie daliście nam długo czekać na odpowiedź. Jesteśmy, bowiem, bardzo zaniepokojeni, gdy zwlekacie z odpowiedzią i zostawiacie nas na różnych domysłach i poszycia. Moi drodzy, pisałam Wam w poprzednim moim liście, że z końcem tego miesiąca, względnie z początkiem przyszłego wybieram się ostatecznie wyjechać. Nie zrealizowałam swego zamiaru, gdyż w moich postanowieniach zaszły różne, nieprzewidziane zmiany.

Otóż narazie jeszcze nie wyjeżdżam, przezimuję w Niemczech, a z wiosną może znowu zajdzie coś nowego tak, że nie mogę Wam napisać ostatecznego mego postanowienia.

Nasunęła się nam możliwość wyjazdu do "wujka Weinberga" On chce wszelkiemi siłami nam dopomóc, nie szczędząc wydatków i kosztów Zdecydowałybym się tam wyjechać, gdyby, naturalnie nie trzeba było długo na to czekać. Krenty, czekamy z niecierpliwością ostatecznych decyzyj stamtąd i co nam czas przyniesie.

Myślę, że chwilowo byłoby nie źle tam wyjechać, zwłaszcza gdy ma się do kogo jechać, kto pomoże w pierwszych, najgorszych chwilach. Drogi Kubo! Jak Ty się na to zapatrujesz? Napisz wszystko szczerze! Nie krępuj się! Wypowiadaj swoje mądre zdanie.

Gdyby w międzyczasie zaszło coś innego (gdyż co do tego nie ma

się 100°/o-wej pewności), to Was natychmiast zawiadomimy i jedno-
cześnie zawiadomimy Was o dniu naszego wyjazdu do Hajf.
zarazie pracujemy obie, przeszukamy, co tylko jest możliwem.
Kupiliśmy już dużo, niezbędnych nam rzeczy. Czekamy dalej,
co nam los zykuje.
Tak, moi kochani, do wszystkiego potrzeba dużo cierpliwości i czekania.
Wiecie Milne jak strasznie pragnę się już spotkać z Wami, z jakiem
stęsknieniem czekam tej ogromnie szczęśliwej dla mnie chwili,
i tu znów muszę się ubroić w cierpliwość i czekać......
Całe życie tylko czekać i dążyć, całe życie i co dalej?
Starzejemy się, życie i młodość ucieka przed nami. To jest naprawdę
okropne. Podrasta nowe pokolenie. Moi dwaj synowie to są
już duże chłopcy. Boruch ma już 4 lata skończonych, Aronkowi
spełnić się 1½ roku. Dzieci są kochane, mądre, chociaż, jak
chłopcy ogromnie tolerzy Najważniejsze jednak, że są zdrowe i dobrze
się rozwijają. Niczego Im nie żałujemy, niczego Im też nie brak.
Patrzę się na te moje bobaski, i kiedy płaczą, wspominając naszą
kochaną mamusię, którą się tak ogromnie cieszyła temi wnukami.
Ale niestety! Trudno wszędzie o tem razem myśleć. Jakby mi było dobrze
nigdy już nie była szczęśliwą, chcę tylko na myśl o naszej tragedii.
Moi kochani! Napisałam Wam o wszystkiem, co Was najbardziej
interesuje. Proszę Was, napiszcie o sobie. Jak Wasze zdrowie?
Jak Wam idzie praca? Co porabia Wasz kochany Daniczek?
Jak On się uczy w szkole? Co słychać nowego?
Kiedy widujecie się z Joskiem i Manią? Co jest z Mundkiem?
Czy przychodzi czasem do Was? O wszystkiem proszę Was, mi napisac.
Rozum już badźcie zdrowi. Całuję Was mocno dużo razy. Jakub
i dzieci ślą Wam we całusów i pozdrowień. Pozdrówcie serdecznie Joska
i Manię Napisze do nich wkrótce. Albo drogę Napisz, lub dopisz sama do mnie
Proszę o najrychlejszą odpowiedź. Wasze oddane dzieci

Ulm, January 25, 1949

My Dear and Beloved!

We got your letter that you sent on January 6th. We received it yesterday and I am writing you back right away. I thank you so much that you did not make us wait too long for your response. We get worried if we do not hear from you for long periods of time.[36]

My dear, as I wrote in a previous letter, at the end of this month or the beginning of the next month I am planning to leave. My plans changed due to unexpected circumstances. Well, I'm not leaving yet, and we will stay throughout the winter in Germany. Hopefully nothing will happen. I will let you know in the spring about my final decision. There is one possibility that we will leave and stay with "Uncle Weinberg."[37] He is trying very hard to help us without sparing anything. He would cover all of the expenses. We would decide to go there (to the U.S.A.) only if we didn't have to wait too long of course.

---

36 After the war, my grandmother's only living relatives were her brother Yaakov "Kuba" Gun, his wife Elza and their son Dani, as well as a first cousin, Yosef Zaltz. All other blood relatives from her entire extended family were murdered by Ukrainian guards and the SS paramilitary death squads known as the Einsatzgruppen (*Einsatzgruppen der Sicherheitspolizei und des SD*). Thus, it is not surprising that she expressed her concern when not hearing from her remaining family members for long periods of time.

37 Uncle Hersh Weinberg lived in America and had left Europe before the start of the war. He was the brother of Devorah Weinberg, mother of my grandfather, Yaakov (Jack) Weinberg. At the time, immigrants needed a sponsor to come to the United States. Since Hersh Weinberg was a United States citizen, he was legally permitted to be a sponsor. Hersh Weinberg was married to a woman who was related to the Hassenfeld family from Providence, Rhode Island. The Hassenfeld family, who later changed their name to Hasboro, was influential in William Henry Vanderbilt III's winning the Rhode Island gubernatorial race in 1938. To show his appreciation, Governor Vanderbilt gave Hersh Weinberg an opportunity to bring over relatives from Europe and after the war, Hersh sponsored the immigration of my grandparents, father, and uncle to the United States.

We are waiting patiently for all the decisions from there. Time will tell what will happen. I think it would be okay to go there temporarily. Besides he is willing to help us.

Dear Kuba, what is your take on this matter? Just be honest! Is this a smart move?[38] There is a possibility that something else will happen. We are not 100% sure about anything. We will notify you right away about changes and about the day of our arrival in Haifa.[39] For now we are working on trying to save whatever we can. We bought a lot of necessary things and we are waiting to see what the future will bring. Yes my dear, we must have lots of patience as we continue to wait. You know how desperately I want to see you all. I miss you so much and seeing you would be the happiest moment of my life. But we have to be patient and wait . . . . This is life, waiting, aspirations and what's next? We are getting older and youth is running away from us. This is so sad.

However, the new generation is growing. My two boys are getting bigger. Boruch[40] is four years old and Arenek[41] is now one and a half. The kids are darlings and smart, but just like boys, full of mischief. The most important thing is that they are healthy. We care for them really well and they have everything. Looking at my little cuties I often cry remembering my beloved mother, who would have enjoyed her grandsons so much. Unfortunately, it is even too hard for me to think about. I feel like I could never be happy because I continuously think about our tragedy.

My dear, I wrote about everything that you may be interested in. Please write to me about your life. How is your dear Daniczck?[42] How is he doing in school? What is new with you? Do you see Josek and

---

[38] 1949 was a difficult economic time for Israel. Kuba Gun discouraged my grandmother from coming to Israel and advised her to go straight to America where there would be opportunity for work.

[39] The plan was for their ultimate arrival in Israel where both brother and sister would be reunited. It appeared that any time spent in America would have been temporary.

[40] Boruch refers to Bernard Weinberg, my father.

[41] Arenek is the Polish Jewish nickname for my uncle Aaron Weinberg.

[42] Dani Gun. He is the son of Kuba who moved to Haifa where he married his second wife, Tova.

Mania[43] sometimes? What's new with Munolek,[44] does he come by sometimes?

Please write to me soon about everything and stay healthy. I am sending all my love. Jakob and the kids are sending kisses to you all. Send my kind regards to Josek and Mania. I will write them separately. Elza, my dear, write back as soon as possible.

Yours,
Lena

---

[43]   Josek is Yosef Zaltz, first cousin to my grandmother, and Mania is his wife.

[44]   A pre-war friend of my grandmother.

| Chapter Nine |

THE LAND OF THE FREE

The journey to America was an uneventful one. The young Weinberg family sailed out of the shipyard in Bremen-Hafen (Bremerhaven), Germany, a small town completely destroyed by Allied forces after they bombed the harbor. The General McRae, a military transport trip, took the refugees to America to start a new life. On board the ship, men and women slept on different floors. Baruch Chaim and Aaron Asher, ages five and two respectively, stayed with their mother for the duration of the one week trip. There were many who became seasick throughout the journey and my grandmother recalled the putrid smell of burnt eggs that permeated the decks of the ship.

USNS General J. H. McRae

TRIPLICATE
(To be given to declarant when originally issued; to be made a part of the petition for naturalization when petition is filed; and to be retained as a part of the petition in the records of the court)

UNITED STATES OF AMERICA

DECLARATION OF INTENTION
(Invalid for all purposes seven years after the date hereof)

No. 367504

STATE OF NEW YORK

EASTERN DISTRICT OF NEW YORK

In the .... DISTRICT .... Court

of ...... UNITED STATES at BROOKLYN, N. Y.

(1) My full, true, and correct name is ...... HELENA WEINBERG

(2) My present place of residence is ...... 113 Amboy Street, Brooklyn, Kings, New York

(3) My occupation is ...... Nurse ...... (4) I am ...... 35 ...... years old. (5) I was born on ...... April 1, 1914

in ...... Krzemieniec, Poland ...... (6) My personal description is as follows: Sex ...... Female

color White complexion Fair, color of eyes Brown color of hair Brown height 5 feet 5 inches, weight 135 pounds

visible distinctive marks ...... None ...... race ...... White, present nationality ...... Stateless

(7) I am ...... married; the name of my ...... husband is ...... Jakob ...... we were married on 1/1/42

at Samarkant, Russia ...... he or she was born at ...... Krakow, Poland

on June 15, 1916 ...... and entered the United States at New York, New York

on November 25, 1949 for permanent residence in the United States, and now resides 113 Amboy St, Bklyn, N

(8) I have ...... 2 ...... children; and the name, sex, date and place of birth, and present place of residence of each of said children who is living, are as follows:

Boruch (M) November 15, 1944, Aaron (M) July 15, 1947, Boruch born in Samarkant, Russia, Aaron born in Ulm, Germany, Both now reside in New York.

(9) My last place of foreign residence was ...... Ulm, Germany ...... (10) I emigrated to the United States from

Bremen, Germany ...... (11) My lawful entry for permanent residence in the United States wa

at New York, New York ...... under the name of Helena Weinberg

on November 25, 1949 ...... on the USAT General J. H. Mc Rae

(12) Since my lawful entry for permanent residence I have not been absent from the United States, for a period or periods of 6 months or longer, as follows:

	DEPARTED FROM THE UNITED STATES			RETURNED TO THE UNITED STATES	
PORT	DATE (Month, day, year)	VESSEL OR OTHER MEANS OF CONVEYANCE	PORT	DATE (Month, day, year)	VESSEL OR OTHER MEANS OF CONVEYANCE

(13) I have not heretofore made declaration of intention: No. ...... on ...... at ...... in the ......

(14) It is my intention in good faith to become a citizen of the United States and to reside permanently therein. (15) I will, before being admitted to citizenship renounce absolutely and forever all allegiance and fidelity to any foreign prince, potentate, state, or sovereignty of whom or which at the time of admission to citizenship I may be a subject or citizen. (16) I am not an anarchist; nor a believer in the unlawful damage, injury, or destruction of property, or sabotage; nor a disbeliever in or opposed to organized government; nor a member of or affiliated with any organization or body of persons teaching disbelief in or opposition to organized government. (17) I certify that the photograph affixed to the duplicate and triplicate hereof is a likeness of me and was signed by me. I do swear (affirm) that the statements I have made and the intentions I have expressed in this declaration of intention subscribed by me are true to the best of my knowledge and belief: SO HELP ME GOD.

Helena Weinberg

Subscribed and sworn to (affirmed) before me in the form of oath shown above in the office of the Clerk of said Court, at ...... Brooklyn, New York

this ...... 4th ...... day of ...... April ...... anno Domini 19 50 I hereby certify that the Certification No. 0300-K-135680 from the Commissioner of Immigration and Naturalization showing the lawful entry for permanent residence of the declarant above named on the date stated in this declaration of intention, has been received by me, and that the photograph affixed to the duplicate and triplicate hereof is a likeness of the declarant.

[SEAL]

Helena Weinberg

DEPUTY Clerk of the U. S. District ...... Court.

By ...... Deputy Clerk.

Form N-315

U. S. DEPARTMENT OF JUSTICE
IMMIGRATION AND NATURALIZATION SERVICE
(Edition of 11-1-41)

16—10119-1   U. S. GOVERNMENT PRINTING OFFICE

It was God's will that we immigrated to the United States. I was very happy. Here I could build a new life and raise my children in this free and wonderful country. Maybe here, I thought, I would forget the past with all its horror. But, after a while I became restless again. I didn't have patience to work. The nightmares didn't allow me to sleep. I always cried and screamed in the nights while endlessly running away from the Germans and Russians in my head. It's always with me. It doesn't let me forget. I will be haunted with terror for the rest of my life.

The Weinberg family arrived at New York Harbor on November 24, 1949, Thanksgiving Day. They were immediately struck by the sounds and smells, but most of all by the lights. Having come from the German town of Bremen-Hafen, which had been completely leveled by the Allied bombers, there were no lights at night. The glitter and shimmer of the New York City skyline was a dream and realization of new hope and opportunity. And with that they began their life anew in a foreign country, without working knowledge of the culture or language. They moved to 113 Amboy Street in the Brownsville section of Brooklyn and began picking up the shattered pieces of a broken past.

Baruch Chaim (Bernard) and Aaron Asher (Aaron) spoke only Yiddish. They had to learn a new language and make friends with children who were born in America and who often looked down on the war ravaged immigrants. Nonetheless, the family remained focused on their goal of integrating into society and creating a new life.

Shortly after coming to America, my grandmother sought to utilize her talent of writing and put it to good use. The editors of the Forward, a daily Yiddish paper, sponsored a contest for new immigrants, asking them to write about their feelings for their new home, America. My grandmother's heartfelt submission was the winning entry. The following is a copy of the letter she wrote to the editors including her submission to the contest as well as her request to become a featured contributor to the paper. The boldfaced selections in this letter are the exact excerpts that were entered as her submission. They are the words of a broken woman expressing her gratitude for the freedoms and safety afforded to her by the United States of America . . .

New York, April 12, 1950

Very Esteemed Editor!

With my arrival in America, I immediately became one of the most devoted readers of your beloved newspaper, the *"Forverts"* (Forward). I am filled with enthusiasm by the articles that are printed there. The freedom of expression and the various problems expressed therein, the open critique, and the resounding Yiddish word capture my heart.

I would be very pleased to become one of your contributors and I believe that I would bring many interesting contributions to this newspaper.

Now, having noticed your appeal to the new immigrants, that they should write letters about their life experiences and related matters, in conjunction with "America, My New Home," I am very gladly doing just that, and writing my letter. I am writing briefly, providing only a single overview of my very difficult, but very interesting and captivating, life experiences because I need to contain myself and write tersely.

A few weeks ago, I began to write my diary, my experiences during the time of the war; that is to say, from 1933 until the time I came to America. I am writing slowly, as I do not want to overlook a single moment, any single small detail of that which I lived through during the course of six difficult, bloody years in Soviet Russia. Up until the present moment, I was forced to remain silent. I hid deeply within myself every feeling and every wish to express myself before all. Now I am in America. My dream of many years has become a reality, the most beautiful one of my life - freedom.

I remember it as if it were now, the outbreak of the Second World War, when I was torn away from my home and fell into the hands of the German murderers. It is difficult to describe how much pain I lived through then at the hands of the murderers, and how much terror and fear as well. I saw that death was encroaching nearer and nearer, that they were building ghettos and death camps, and that it would be impossible to survive the war. I then risked my life and fled to the Russians, who had conquered the other part of Poland (Poland was then divided by the San River into two parts; one belonged to

the Germans and the other to the Russians). I fled to the liberators, to the joyousness of freedom and humanity, to the place where my former home was. But it's unbelievable! For crossing the border, the Russians dragged me toward them, far into Russia, taking us like animals in barred wagons that resounded terrifyingly with the heavy lock of the door on the opposite side of the wagon. They promised us that they had no prisons there, that we would only work, that they would take us to a new place of residence, and that we would then be free people, and live in a very beautiful, free land. But in their devilish faces, the great lie, which rang throughout their entire Stalin-Land, was reflected. I myself saw a terrifying "prison," the well-known Odessa jail with its tens of cellblocks for thousands of prisoners, for thousands of innocent people. That was supposed to be my house of betterment,[45] my education. The prison, that was packed full of so many people from all over the world, was supposed to be the so-called warm home. What an irony of fate!

I spent 18 months there in pain and in suffering. I will never forget the terrifying nights during which they would schlep me in for interrogations. I observed the suffering of wealthy Russians with prison sentences of 10-15-20 years. My heart ached for them. My heart understood, looking at the little children, who also found their houses of embitterment within this very same prison. I also suffered for my beloved, for whom my heart so painfully longed. I also longed for freedom, for the most beautiful and humane life. But I was forced to suffer, and yet again, to suffer; and deep within myself, I gathered together everything that I witnessed there. I wanted to live, I wanted to scream out to the world the entire truth, the hurt and rage that came with red Communism. I received a sentence of five years, having been sent from Moscow without a court and without a defense. I was deported to do forced labor in distant Siberia. Then, in the camps, I was able to meet other people, also people who had been deported.

I would speak with them quietly; I heard thousands of tragedies. They would ask me with tears in their eyes, that at the first opportunity, I should let the world know their tragedy, help them. I would promise them that the heart understands. Alas, we did not

---

[45]   This is a literal translation from the Yiddish expression used in the original letter. This same phrase will reappear in this letter.

know that. The Russian people were good, but the regime - the cursed red regime . . . I saw my entire life in Soviet Russia, both in captivity and as a free person. I will immortalize this in my diary. When I remember all of the dark days, my entire body shakes, and I am unable to compose myself. The tragic moments swim before my eyes, but I am fortunate that I can now write about it candidly and freely.

I am in America for a short time, only four months. I am fortunate that I can live in such a free, democratic land. I move boldly across the streets; I am not afraid to look around, that they will drag me off and enslave me. I left behind the terrible Russian soil, which administered all sorts of means of destroying the human spirit and belief. I left behind the bloody German soil, which destroyed millions of human lives.

My family and I were brought with the help of "HIAS"[46] **to America. I quivered from joy, once I was already aboard the ship that brought me here. She shook, and my thoughts drew me into the distance. I thought about my future, about how I would establish myself, and how I would adjust to the new life that stood before me. But more and more, my heart became enlivened with the thought that I am a free person, and that I will be able with my free will to build a home here. The curiosity to be all of these things that one relates about the golden land wouldn't budge from within me. Ultimately, the day came. We arrived in New York harbor. Our relatives met us with warm words, reassured us that we would feel good here, that we would settle down and live happily. The warm words were far dearer than the hundreds of dollars that other people receive from their relatives.**

We will - my husband and I - build our home. "HIAS" provided us with our initial help; we are very grateful to them. We are happy about every little thing that creates a feeling of freedom.

There are moments when my terrible past appears before my eyes, and for that reason, I love my current life twice as much. We settled down quickly here, the main thing being - finding an apartment for ourselves. My husband began working. And although the work is difficult and not his trade (because he is an

---

[46] Hebrew Immigrant Aid Society.

electrician), we are, however, happy that we can independently stand on our own two feet. We live with the hope that the future will be even more beautiful and better.

I love my new home - America. Here I have found everything toward which I had aspired - "Freedom." I will learn the English language, which will help me overcome all the difficulties and become acclimated more easily. My husband and I will gladly serve the country. We will teach both of our children love for the country, in which they have a future for themselves.

With an upraised head, with gratitude in our teary eyes, and with an enlivened heart, I have high esteem for you, America, my new land, and lay before your feet, springtime flowers, which convey a symbol of love and freedom.

Just as we teach our two children love for our Jewish people and for our Jewish land, so too, we will teach them: She stands out with her vastness, for within her beats the pulse of freedom, and a free, beautiful life.

The Vastness of America, "My New Home" of New York

One wonderfully beautiful land is America. This is the land to which I aspired with my entire desire and all of my wishes and my youth. In this land, the sun lights up with all of her light, brilliant rays. She is happy when she approaches, she laughs along with everyone, for this is a land of light and a land of scholarship, a land that brings with it joy in life, freedom, and happiness.

There, in contrast, in Europe, from which the sun approaches, there is darkness and tears. There one finds enslavement; there one finds murder, and the spilling of innocent blood.

America is yet very young. She was only discovered 500 years ago, but she progressed, she blossomed. Just like the beautiful month of May and nature, the most beautiful ideas and hopes continue to bloom here. Freedom, democracy, and the struggle for a beautiful life for everyone and for everything blooms here.

There, in contrast, whence we hail, from across the ocean, what has the world achieved? It regressed, with its terrible, medieval slogan, "The right of the mighty" (i.e., "Might makes right").

There was a return to the cruel times of Nero,[47] of inquisitions, to the command of leaders who only wanted to throw all of mankind before their feet. They wanted to destroy everything that is beautiful, cultured, and humane. That soil gave rise to Hitler, Stalin, Mussolini - murderers, dreamers of power over human troops, over human blood and suffering. But here, people marvel at the beautiful land - America, the land of Lincoln, Washington, Roosevelt, and Truman - people with ideals, crusaders for a more beautiful future for humanity.

I marvel at this land of America, which has now become my new home. Following long years of wandering, which were laden with the terrible suffering - both from the perspective of the Hitler-Land, as well as from the perspective of the Stalin-Land - I have, indeed, aspired to this land, in which I am building my new home. I have thrown away my wanderer's staff, and have come ashore. My heart is yet full of sorrow for all of my loved ones who perished under such horrible means in the gas ovens. I still long for my former, good home in which I lived my young, unforgettable years. Nothing can render all of that, but life goes on, and the struggle for life is strong - especially, since I am not alone, but with a man and our two little children - for whom I must and want to create a beautiful future.

I am now in the largest city in America, in New York, which basks in the thousands of lights of advertisements, beautiful performances, cinemas, theaters, museums, and so forth. She stands out with her vastness. For how beautiful the childish voices sound when the children run to school to learn. They are happy and fortunate that they live in such a beautiful land in which one educates and develops their young souls with the best ideas of love for humanity. However, look at "Hitler's" children! Their hearts were from the beginning already poisoned with hatred and brutality toward other people.

So, you newly arrived in America, do say, is it not to behold the vastness of the land, which is in reality, greater than all the other lands

---

[47] Nero (54-68) was a Roman emperor who was known for his tyranny and extravagance and is infamously credited with "fiddling while Rome burned." Given this background, the personality of Nero appears well-matched to the cruel, medieval times to which my grandmother alludes.

of the world? And everyone must learn from them what a beautiful life is. Yes, I am fortunate that I live here, in America. I have a future for myself. My children now have a future, for everything is attainable for them here, even the greatest centers of culture.

We are slowly becoming rooted in this new ground . . .

May a new life blossom. The beginning is difficult, perhaps very difficult, but with time, everything will become easier.

Experiences make for scholarship. That is what one proverb says. We already know everything about life. For us, nothing is difficult. The 10 years since the outbreak of the Second World War, experiences and hardships, opened up our eyes to everything. We are not *grinne* ("greenhorns"), as they call us; life has already grounded us, made us aware of all the hardest problems - perhaps far more so than the local, native-born Americans. Not knowing the English language also creates many problems for us in becoming settled and finding a good place for ourselves in which to work. But everything will quickly be relegated to the past, for the great desire to create, to live, and to build a beautiful home for ourselves will conquer all the difficulties.

I call out to you, my brothers, to you, new immigrants, that you not lose courage, the hope that the future must indeed be more beautiful and better. Go to work driven, and also add a brick to the subsequent construction of the beautiful, great structure which represents the beautiful, wonderful land of America.

Weinberg family celebrating their first Passover in New York

„אַמעריקע מײַן נײַע הײם"

(שלום פון בינטעל־בריף פעידוש)

טעך סוירוויס פאר ניו אמעריקענס"
פאר דער הילף וואס זיי האבען אונז
געגעבען.

די אידען אין פילאַדעלפיע האבען אים גוט אויפגענומען

(קאָנטעסט־בריף)

פון אייזיק באָרענשטיין

אין מאנאט דעצעמבער, 1949, בין
איך מיט מיין פאמיליע, נאך צען יאר
זיין נע־ונד, ענדליך אנגעקימען אין
פילאַדעלפיע, וואו די „דזשואיש פעמי־
לי סוירווים" האט זיך מיט אונז פאר־
אינטערעסירט און באַזארגט, אז מיר
זאלען זיך קענען באלד איינאָרדענען.
עטליכע טעג שפעטער האב איך ביי־
נאכט באקומען א הארץ־אטאקע. מיין
בעל־הבית'טע האט טעלעפאנירט נאך
דעם דאקטאר יעראמע קאהן, וועלכער
איז באלד געקומען און איז ביז 3
ביינאכט געווען ביי מיר און דערנאך
גאנצע זעקס וואכען טעגליך מיך באַ־
זוכט אין האספיטאל צוזאמען מיט דר.
פישער. פאר דער גאנצער צייט האָ־
בען זיי ניט געוואלט נעמען ביי מיר
קיין געלט, פאר וואס איך וויל זיי
ביי דער געלעגענהייט אויסדריקען מיין
הארציליכסטען דאנק פאר זייער מיה
און ארבייט מיך צוריק געזונט צו
מאכען.
די שכנים פון דער הויז, וואו
איך וואוין, פארזארגען מיך מיט
מיין פאמיליע מיט אלעם וואס מיר
נויטיגען זיך אין שטוב. וואו מיר
קומען נאר, ווייזט מען אונז ארויס
גרויס פריינדליכקייט און מען פאר־
זארגט אונז מיט אלץ וואס מיר
נויטיגען זיך.
מיר קענען זיין שטאלץ מיט אונזע־
רע פילאַדעלפיער אידען; זיי קענען
דינען ווי א מוסטער פאר אנדערע
אידען אין אנדערע שטעט ווי זיך צו
באציען צו די „גרינע".

די ווארימע ווערטער פון די קרובים זיינען ביי איך געווען מער ווי געלט

(קאָנטעסט־בריף)

פון העלענאַ ווייגבערג

איך בין אין אמעריקע בלויז פיר
מאנאטען. איך בין גליקליך וואס איך
קען לעבען אין אזא פרייען, דעמאָ־
קראטישען לאנד, וואו איך גיי דרייסט
איבער די גאסען אהן שרעק זיך ארומ־
צוקוקען, אז אט וועט מען מיך פאר־
שלעפען און פארשקלאפען, ווי אויף
דער רוסישער ערד, וואו מען פארניכ־
טעט דעם מענשליכען גייסט און גלויי־
בען; ווי אויף דער בלוטיגער דויי־
טשער ערד, אויף וועלכער מ'האט פאר־
ניכטעט מיליאנען מענשליכע לעבענס.
איך מיט מיין פאמיליע זיינען גע־
בראכט געווארען קיין אמעריקע מיט
דער הילף פון „האיאס". איך האב גע־
ציטערט פון פרייד ווען איך בין שוין
געווען אויף דער שיף, וועלכע האט
מיך געפירט אהער. ווען מיר זיינען
אנגעקומען אין ניו יארקער האפען,
האבען אונז באגעגענט אונזערע
קרובים און מיט ווארימע ווערטער
אונז פארזיכערט אז מיר וועלען זיך
דא פילען גוט. די ווארימע ווערטער
זיינען געווען פיל טייערער ווי די הונ־
דערטער דאלאר וואס אנדערע האבען
באקומען פון זייערע קרובים.
דער „האיאס" האט אונז געגעבען
די ערשטע הילף, פארוואס מיר זיינען
אים זעהר דאנקבאר. מיר פרייען זיך
מיט יעדער קליינינקייט וואס שאפט
דעם געפיל פון פרייהייט.
עס זיינען פאראן מאמענטען, ווען
עס באוויזט זיך פאר די אויגען די
שרעקליכע פארגאנגענהייט און דארום
איז דאפעלט ליב פאר מיר דאס איצ־
טיגע לעבען. מיר האבען זיך דא שנעל
איינגעאָרדענט און האפען צו געפינען
פאר זיך א וואוינונג. מיין מאן האט
אנגעפאנגען צו ארבייטען, און כאטש
די ארבייט איז א שווערע און ניט פון
זיין פאך (ער איז אן עלעקטרישען),
זיינען מיר אבער צופרידען וואס מיר
קענען זיך זעלבסטשטענדיג שטעלען
אויף די פיס. מיר לעבען מיט האפ־
נונג, אז די צוקונפט וועט זיין אלץ
שענער און בעסער.
איך האב ליב מיין נייע היים —
אמעריקע. איך האב געפונען דא אלץ
צו וואס איך האב געשטרעבט — די
פרייהייט. איך וועל זיך לערנען די
ענגלישע שפראך, וועלכע וועט מיר
העלפען ביייקומען אלע שוועריגקייטען
און לייכטער זיך איינאָרדנען. איך
מיט מיין מאן וועלען ארבייטען פאר
דעם לאנד. אזוי ווי מיר לערנען אונ־
זערע צוויי קינדער ליבשאפט צו אונ־
זער אידיש פאלק, אזוי וועלען מיר
זיי לערנען ליבשאפט צו דעם לאנד,
אין וועלכען זיי האבען פאר זיך א
צוקונפט.

The actual Forward newspaper from 1950

JEWISH DAILY FORWARD
World's Largest Jewish Daily
175 EAST BROADWAY
NEW YORK 2, N.Y.

דעם 13טן יולי, 1950

י. ווײנבערג
113 אמבאי סטריט
ברוקלין, נ.י.

ליבער פריינד ווײנבערג:

בײגעלײגט געפינט איהר א טשעק אויף דער סומע פון 10$.

דאָס איז דער פרייז פאר אייער קאָנטעסט-בריף אויף דער טעמע:
"אַמעריקע - מיין ניי היים", וואָס איז געווען געדרוקט אין "פאָר-
ווערטס".

מיר שיקען איך אויך צוריק אייער בילד, ווי איהר האָט פאַר-
לאַנגט.

מיט פריינדליכען גרוס,

קאָנטעסט קאָמיטעט

בײ:
ימ/חג

FORWARD BUILDING
CHICAGO, ILL.

THE GATEWAY TO THE JEWISH MARKET

July 13, 1950

Dearest Weinberg Friend,

Enclosed please find a check for the sum of $10.

This is the prize for our contest on the topic of "America - My New Home", which was published in the Forwards.

We are also sending you back your picture as you requested.

With Friendly Regards,
Contest Committee

Chapter Ten

WHAT IS HAPPINESS

God created the world with love and he gave it to the people with love. His tendency is to make people happy. There are those people that don't understand what happiness is and they ruined happiness for others from the beginning of their existence. Happiness is joy and peace that we feel inside. It is a warm feeling full of love and beauty. We are happy when we are satisfied with what we have in life. Some people are born to be happy; as they say, "this person was born under a happy star." But everyone can build his own happiness with strength just like the proverb says, "Every man is a smith of his own happiness."

Real happiness is found when shared with others. If one is fortunate to be rich and shares his wealth with others, his reward is happiness. One finds happiness by bringing help, love, understanding and hope to sick, suffering and hopeless people. The greatest happiness goes along with having warm feelings for the whole world.

We each find happiness in different ways. Some people are happy when they are skilled in some way and are able to develop their talents either in music, writing, acting, business or in creating things, which are favored for themselves and for humanity. Some people are happy when they live on the bosom of nature, like farmers. They are full of joy and happiness listening to the singing birds and feeling the coolness of fresh soil and the smell of blooming trees surrounded by nature's beauty in every season of the year.

There are people who are happy only in their youth, which is of course the happiest and the most beautiful season of our lives. But some people are happy in every season of their life even in their oldest age when life is so close to its end.

We are happy when we are healthy, especially after recovering from a long and serious sickness and we are able again to go on with our duties. How happy are those who win back their freedom after they lost if for a long time. Health, freedom, and peace combine together to form happiness.

Just as there are happy individuals, there are happy nations. While living the principles of a democracy; liberty, freedom and peace, there is happiness. Those nations are satisfied with everything they possess, not desiring other people's property. On the contrary, they share their goods with others. Our United States is one of those countries, which is happy to share its goods and to help so many countries in the world while respecting everyone's independence and personal freedom. This is democracy at its highest point. The Unites States made great efforts during World War Two to save so many people from the concentration camps in Germany, sharing their bread and clothing and helping those needy people in every possible way to feel happy.

There is no happiness in a country under a dictatorship where there is no respect for personal freedom. There is no happiness in Russia whose main goal is to conquer the world and make everyone slaves. There is no happiness in today's world. We all starve for peace but there is no peace. We heard so often the terrible word "war" and we are frightened because war could mean the end of our existence.

How different the world would be if it were built on happiness and everyone would know and understand the meaning of this great word.

Chapter Eleven

I CANNOT FORGET YOU, MY KREMENITZ

New York, February 23, 1953

Like a dream, 14 years have passed since I last left my beloved city, Kremenitz. Many years have gone by, years of pain and struggle. Difficult, sorrowful years, perhaps the worst years of my life.

Perhaps a bitter foreshadowing filled my heart with the knowledge that I was seeing my beloved city for the last time. One cannot ever forget Kremenitz, the lush, beautiful city, with her wonderfully beautiful nature, with her dear and beloved people, in which beat the pulse of a Jewish heart. I still love you even today, my beautiful Kremenitz. I long for you day and night, and I can never stop feeling sorrowful about my most beloved and dear ones, whom the cursed German devil so frighteningly murdered. Oft-times my thoughts carry me back to the distant past, to a world of memories, to a world of dreams, to a more beautiful and better world, which no longer exists, but still exists, buried in the deepest corners of my soul. And so I see how, in reality, our city Kremenitz was arranged with her small houses, in a small valley, and how around and around her wove the hands of the wonderfully beautiful mountains.

Who from among us, Kremenitzer, doesn't recall the indescribable beauty of the city, in which nature, with her paint brush, sketched out an enchanted picture with thousands of shades and colors? The

greatest artist would not be able to capture so many shades and so much beauty, as nature had managed to do. I see my city in her springtime splendor, abloom, and dressed in her green dresses, woven through with the various colors of flowers, which give off aromatic fragrances. I see my city in the rich, golden autumn, and in the white winter nights, wrapped in her sparkling snow robe, like an enchanted queen. And today, around and around, the fields and woods filled with the singing of birds, and with the buzzing of bees and flies.

People came from all over the world to marvel at the rich beauty of our Kremenitz, which we crowned with the name, "The Wolyner Switzerland."[48] And all those who visited the city were unable to absorb the surrounding beauty with their glance. It was here that the queen of the mountains [i.e., Kremenitz], the "Bona,"[49] with her old ruins from the former fortress, in which the Polish Queen "Bona" once lived, and, according to one legend, died. And in addition, the "Da Vinci" Girl Mountains,[50] the "Black," and the "Chalky" Mountains;[51] and from one side, the beautiful gorge wove itself around Kremenitz, as with the "Królewski Most" - the royal bridge. And the fragrant evergreen woods stretched further, through Brzeziec and Pochayiv, even further, and more beautiful. Nature wove her beautiful carpet, upon which various sounds mixed with the songs of birds and the flowing of the river waves, and the buzzing of bees, and the aching of swaying trees resounded. A godly melody and an enchanted landscape. Everything lived within nature. Everything sang out a beautiful, beloved city - Kremenitz!

---

[48] Kremenitz (or Krzemieniec) is located in a region that was once referred to as Wolyn in Polish, "Volhin" in Yiddish.

[49] This is a reference to Queen Bona Sforza (1493-1557) with whose name the Bona Castle is associated.

[50] "Da Vinci's Girl" is an allusion to a painting the noted artist made, entitled "Lady with an Ermine." This painting, which is found in the Wawel Castle, in Krakow, Poland, is considered by some to be the most precious painting in the country's possession.

[51] The terms translated here mean "Black" and "Chalky," and are based on Polish words that appear in the original Yiddish text. These words have been capitalized, because it appears that they may have been used as names for actual regional mountains, or quite likely, colloquially.

The rushing streets of Kremenitz were feverish with life. A Jewish heart possessed our Kremenitz. Branched-out families drew their roots back several generations. Good, sincere people. Everyone loved one another. Beloved Jewish children streamed into the schools with a great desire to learn, to drink up as much knowledge as possible. Many learned people hailed from our Kremenitz. Doctors and lawyers, engineers and chemists, teachers, and work-specialists. And above all rang the Yiddish word, the Yiddish language, the Yiddish song. We may be genuinely proud that our Kremenitz gave rise to the world famous Isaac Ber Levinsohn,[52] and also, to the great Polish poet, Juliusz Słowacki.[53] How can one forget all of that? Can we forget the years of our childhood blossoming, which we spent together with our dear and beloved parents, sisters, and brothers, relatives, and neighbors? How can we forget the holidays, the joyous occasions, which added an adornment of Jewish charm?

How beautifully laid-out the Great Kremenitz Synagogue was - the crowned edifice for the Jewish population. And the other synagogues in which one prayed so wholeheartedly, and believed so deeply in the Almighty. Every *shtibl*,[54] every little piece of flint, every little curl - how dear all of this was to us, and how much more so, now, when we no longer have it. Everyone - great and small, rich and poor, all of these sincere, beloved forms. Who can forget this? Kremenitz, my Kremenitz, where are you now, where is all of that from once upon a time?

Cities and towns have disappeared, large structures have toppled, and forests have been burnt down. But all of this is nothing. Cities can be built anew, but you, my beloved, who shall rouse you from your eternal slumber? The ground is saturated with your innocent blood. Young lives were cut short, and their bones were scattered far and wide. It has grown quiet in our Kremenitz; quiet, as though at

---

[52] Rabbi Isaac Ber Levinsohn (also spelled Levinson) was known by the acronym *Ribal*, and was considered to be an enlightened thinker in the style of Moses Mendelsohn.

[53] Słowacki (1809-1849) is considered to be one of Poland's great romantic poets. He was born in Kremenitz, which he characterized in his writings as a "paradise lost."

[54] Small synagogue.

a cemetery, where no graves even remain, because the murderer also uprooted that.

A living world was wiped out, a world with song. The heart of our Kremenitz has ceased beating. There is no more Kremenitz. Even the birds have disappeared from the woods, since for whom shall they now sing. Our beloved children are no more; may their song be received. Even the mountains have mournfully lowered their heads.

The ground cries and quivers. She absorbed too much innocent blood. She cannot bear it. Melancholy days envelope the entire city. The deep sorrow cries and screams. For deep, deep, in our hearts there is a bloody, painful and never-to-be-healed wound. Why, why, such a mournful end, for you, my Kremenitz? I long for you, Kremenitz. I long for you, my dear parents, sisters and relatives, and I long for you, Kremenitz. I can never forget you, and I will never forget my beloved city, Kremenitz.

A photograph of the Synagogue in Kremenitz

| Chapter Twelve |

A POETIC TRIBUTE TO KREMENITZ

Nisht Fargesn - Not Forgetting

My *shtetele*[55] Kremenitz
For the love still remains
Forever inside
It reaches across
Through the distance of oceans,
From valleys and forests,
Past all borders and walls
I cannot forget
My dear Kremenitz.
I'm not allowed and I don't want to
forget a single place.
My *shtetele* rises
With the blooming of spring,
Singing and shining
With music and color.
And how can I forget,
The purity and beauty,
The mountains and forests
The meadows, the greenness?
When everything there,

---

[55] A small village in Eastern Europe.

Filled with dreams,
With joy and singing
With childish fantasies.
How wonderfully lovely
was my youth spent there.
I absorbed so much beauty
from the delightful surroundings.
I used to leap through the fields like a fawn,
Resting in the mountains, singing with the birds.
Full of curiosity, I used to frequently greet the sunrise,
When the flowers and grasses were dripping with pearls of dew.
How many times I ran,
In the snow in the rain,
through the narrow streets
The paths and the trails.
It's hard to forget,
It stands before my eyes,
My dear parents,
My sisters and relatives,
So many friends, so many loved ones,
I can feel their gentle caresses
Lucid and real
Their love was so warm.
O, how happy was living,
Flowing among them.
Full of joy and elation.
It's so hard to forget.
So don't ever say,
Kremenitz has vanished.
It is full of our memories
And woven into our lives.
And the innocent blood screams from there,
And pain and suffering pours out.
The wind weeps among the grasses,
Where the ash was poured out.
I think I can also see the tragic image
Of their very last step.
And the echo resonates distantly

Of the sharp sound of their beckoning.
Hours, days and weeks are passing,
Time has swallowed many years.
And all that's left is the longing,
And the sadness still remains.
I would so much like to fulfill,
The dream I've had for many years,
Make them a gravestone, a symbol,
Their voices shall not be forgotten.
Maybe in tomorrow's spring,
Little birds will wander there,
And through singing their songs,
Will sanctify the place.
O, how happy that will make me,
How honored and rich.
I will with joy shout from my heart:
"I have not forgotten you!"

Tsu Mayn Kremenitz - To My Kremenitz

Bells have been rung in the distance,
Filling the world with their sounds,
The tones are gradually fading
As my heart overflows with longing.
My thoughts are wandering quickly,
To a faraway world, to my home,
To a world that has already vanished,
With her purity, beauty and charm.
Day and night the image stands before my eyes,
I am back in my *shtetele,* my Kremenitz,
I feel the wind shaking the trees,
I see the pearls of morning dew.
For my Kremenitz, proud of her beauty,
With the hills locking her in.
The Dzievice, Bone and Tcernce
All links of a single chain.
Far away a ship has blown its horn,
Calling me through the deep dark night,
It has taken my sleep and my rest,
Summoning my heart and my soul.
The moon wandered mystically,
The stars sparkled endlessly,
The wind caressed and beckoned to me:
"Come back, come home to your Kremenitz."
I am enchanted by the dreams,
A new longing is born in my heart,
Tears clog up my throat
And my rest is forever lost.
I let the pain in my heart cry out,
Maybe it will still my longing,
I want to return to my *shtetele,*
And bask in my dreams once again.
I would run among meadows and flowers,
Hugging the trees in the woods,
I would take the hills into my arms,
And right away, I'd feel young.

I would run through all of the alleys,
I loved every single one,
I remember them all, the streets and the houses,
I once lived in one of them.
Every corner is filled with my dreams,
I gave so much of myself to them,
I can never, never forget them,
I will infinitely miss them forever.
My mother's gentle caress
Filled my life with joy,
Every day was like gliding through flowers,
Bursting with beauty and purity.
How many times through the familiar streets,
With packs of books under my arms
Did I hurry to get to my school,
With my dreams hovering in me.
But I can never really return
To Kremenitz, my old home,
My loved ones have all disappeared
Not a trace of them remains.
I cannot come to the silent hills,
They cannot even shed a tear,
I cannot ask the birds of the forest
I cannot learn anything from them.
I have wandered throughout the world,
And finally I have chosen a home,
And though life is full of wonders,
My heart remains in Kremenitz.
The bells continue to ring,
Carrying tones from somewhere,
Silently carrying a longing,
From my home, from my past, from my Kremenitz.

Chapter Thirteen

ROKHELEH

In a brilliant style of expressing loss through the medium of a short story, in this next selection, my grandmother seeks to personalize the tragedy of the loss of her hometown through metaphor. Rokheleh, which was actually the name of her mother, was a name that my grandmother gave to honor her hometown. It is a story which describes life and vigor as well as pain and loss. Towards the end of the story Rokheleh speaks of the disease that will soon take her life. It is a stark imagery of the war that ravaged European Jewry.

At the end of her life, when my grandmother stopped speaking clearly and would go into incoherent rants, she would repeat the same refrain, "incurable disease," over and over again. It was the incurable disease of the destruction of her home and European Jewry that she was unable to comprehend or rectify. She makes it clear that it is only the memories which remain. And while painful as those might be, they are the only lasting remnant and so they must be cherished . . .

"Why so early, Rokheleh?" The Bubbe turned to her grandchild, to a thin, small girl, with the name Rokheleh. Rokheleh felt somewhat guilty that she woke up her Bubbe. After all, it was very early. The day had just begun. It was already quite bright, because it was already June, when the summer is in full bloom and all of nature awakens very early. The golden rays of the big hot sun poured throughout the whole sky and teasingly descended upon the earth, waking everything from the night's sleep. Nature awoke, the birds began to sing, the flies started buzzing and everything was so wonderfully pretty and fresh. More and more, the voices of people began to ring as daily life began again.

Rokheleh sat up in a corner of her Bubbe's big house, her head leaning deeply into her hand, thinking deeply. When her Bubbe repeated the question, she came to, glanced in her Bubbe's direction, and quietly answered: "Oh, Bubbe, I couldn't sleep or rest the whole night. I don't know why . . . my heart is nagging me, it drives me to a place where I cannot find any room. But I didn't want to wake Mother, because she goes to bed so late, so exhausted from the day's work. That is why I came to you, my dear Babusieh. Maybe I will feel better with you." Bubbe became anxious. She quickly put on a dress, and some shoes, and, taking Rokheleh by the hand, led her to her bed, undressed her and tucked her in. Rokheleh lay for a while lost in thought and, it seemed, fell asleep.

Bubbe watched her anxiously from afar and quietly wiped tears from her old eyes. "My child, my poor little lamb, what I have to see in my older years . . ." Rokheleh, her daughter's little girl, was fourteen years old, but she looked no older than eight. She was born just like any other normal child, with two black, shining eyes, and a beautiful head of black hair. Her intelligence and her talents were astonishing. All who saw the little girl were impressed by her abilities of song and dance. At five years old, she already knew all of the latest songs and musical numbers from the theater. Everything was sung with emotion and charm. Her temperament was shaped by her good taste and artistic qualities. She was once invited to a concert to dance ballet. She was dressed in a pretty tutu, and performed a beautiful dance for a large crowd. She was wildly applauded and inundated with flowers and various gifts. "She is turning out to be a child of many talents,"

people said of her, bewildered. Her parents were delighted with their wonderful daughter.

Rokheleh was not an only child. She had a sister and three brothers. All of the children were impressive, but she blew them all out of the water with her intelligence and her talents and, moreover, she was good and loyal to her parents, obeying, loving and appreciating them. More than anything, Rokheleh loved her father. She couldn't wait until the evening, when her father would come home from work and she would jump on him with her little hands, hold him tight and whisper "Tateliu, Tateleh, how I missed you! I love you so much Tateleh!" After eating, Rokheleh crawled onto her father's lap and began to tell him about all of the events of the day, and she laughed and joked.

Oftentimes, people were astounded by her wit. Such a small girl with such mental abilities! She teased everyone, she imitated her friends, how they talk, how they walk, she didn't leave anyone off the hook, she found the humorous flaws in everyone. But no one was offended, because she was so good-natured and she showed deep respect for her elders. Anyway, everyone was already used to her impressions, and all used to laugh with her shrill voice. But all of a sudden, her voice stopped. She suddenly stopped singing and dancing. She distanced herself from people and her pretty, black, wise eyes filled with sadness.

"What's wrong, Rokheleh?" Everyone wondered. "Why don't we see you anymore? Everyone missed you. You know how dull it is without your songs, without your charm?" Rokheleh fell ill. She caught a cold and her lungs became very sensitive. Her coughing exhausted her day in day out, and drew from her all of her energy. The child stopped blooming. Like a flower that just yesterday was blossoming and emitting the fragrance of her delightful beauty and today is suddenly wilting, and no trace remains of yesterday's blooming. A parasite snuck into Rokheleh, an unwelcome worm, which nursed on her body, tortured her night and day, and stole her beautiful, blooming childhood, her youth.

Rokheleh's small body attempted to fight back, struggled with the enemy of her young life, but the enemy was stronger. More and more, her body and her soul sank, more and more, the worm prevailed.

But Rokheleh wants to live. She loves life, she loves the beauty of nature, the birds, the flowers, the sun, everything in the world, even the small creek not far from her house. Doctors are powerless to help her; Rokheleh has tuberculosis. It has spread deeply throughout her two lungs. She fights with all of her power to live every day. When she visits the doctor she asks him questions that tear his heart apart with pain, and tears appear in his eyes. She sees her verdict in his glance and in his voice. She knows that she has received a death sentence, but she fights on, anyway.

"Doctor, help me! I am so young! I don't want to die. Heal me! You see how beautiful the world is! I don't want to leave it behind when I haven't yet lived. I don't want to abandon my parents, my sister, my brothers whom I love so much. Oy, and my father, my beloved father. How will he live without me?" The doctor cannot answer her. When he tries, he stammers with his voice. "Silly girl," he says to comfort her, "you will live and be healthy. Go home, don't think about your disease. Eat and drink and you will soon be healthy." But nothing can help Rokheleh. Not the doctor's words, not the good food, and not even the Sanatorium and the thick, fragrant pine forests. Rokheleh cried silently in the corner, not wanting to inconvenience her parents, sometimes going to her Bubbe to unload her heart. Her parents were suffering day and night, couldn't bear to see the pain of their child without being able to help her. They sent her to the best doctors and got her the best medicine that money could buy. They would have given her years of their own lives, to ensure that she would stay alive. Rokheleh used to speak frequently to her Bubbe. "Bubbe, you know, I would gladly give a foot, a hand, an eye, anything to keep on living in this world. Just look, Bubbe, how children play in the street so happily, like I used to. And I can't even play with them because their mothers forbade them, because I can infect them with my disease." Tears streamed from her extinguished eyes.

Rokheleh no longer blossomed like other children her age. She became a skeleton, thin bones, with transparent skin stretched over them. This is all that remained of Rokheleh at 14 years. She lies now with open eyes barely breathing. The day is hot, the sun burns mercilessly, and Rokheleh is struggling to breathe. She cannot lie still. She is driven from place to place. She is turning and turning, like a

shadow from corner to corner. She looks at her hands, her feet, her body. "Look what has become of me!", she whispers. She constantly looks to the window. "When will my Tateliu come home already?"

Rokheleh is now in bed, now with her mother, now in bed again. She starts doing something, sewing or something, and soon enough, back to bed. She is so anxious today. Is this the end? Father and Mother fool themselves "Maybe a miracle, surely a miracle will happen. Rokheleh can't just die! Mother earth will weep, she doesn't want to swallow such a young girl."

When Rokheleh sees her Bubbe entering, she becomes happier, she is revived: "Bubbe, I will come visit you later. Will you cook beans with broth today? I love eating it at your house. Yes, I will definitely come! Maybe in one hour." One hour later, Rokheleh is lying in her white bed near the window. The sun was about to set. Her final rays caressed Rokheleh's pale, stretched-out face, as if to embrace her for the last time. Rokheleh raised her head. She already couldn't speak, but her wise eyes spoke. Her glance wandered around the whole room. And when she saw her beloved father, her face lit up. She called him over, and hugged him like she used to, with her weak, thin arms. Her father won't let her die, she can rest peacefully now. Rokheleh closed her eyes and fell asleep forever.

| Chapter Fourteen |

FOREVER MY JERUSALEM

June 1963

*A*s the years progressed, my grandparents worked tirelessly to provide a good life for their two sons. They were acclimating to their new home and Bernard and Aaron were excelling in school. Kuba, my grandmother's brother, came to New York for his first and only time for my father's Bar-Mitzvah in November of 1957. This visit brought great joy to my grandmother but she still longed to visit Israel, the land she learned about as a child and dreamt about seeing, especially since the war ended. This dream was finally realized in the summer of 1963 . . .

Kuba and Helen at my father's Bar Mitzvah, November 1957

With a shiver in my heart but full of joy, I boarded the plane that was to take me to our Jewish homeland, Israel. Mixed feelings filled my heart. In a few short hours, my dream will be actualized, my long-sought fantasy to visit the wonderfully pretty land of the *Chumash*.[56] And I will soon meet my beloved brother and his family, with friends and loved ones. On the other hand, I already miss my own family, my husband and children, whom I am abandoning for two long months with only one round of letters to still my longing.

The plane slid and cut through the air high and far away above the earth and brought me further and further away from my home and closer to my goal. The airplane was buzzing with a variety of noises. Different kinds of people: Elderly, adults and very young people, all with different purposes for their trips to Israel. Some were coming for the first time, some for the second or third time, but all had the same feeling of pride and love for the Jewish state.

We landed peacefully in Lod, Israel's main airport. I was still in my own world when I found myself in my brother's arms along with his wife and son. I am shedding tears of joy. I am enveloped in a *heimish*[57] and warm atmosphere, the sound of Hebrew language and a feeling of utmost pride that this is all ours. It belongs to the Jewish people and I am coming home, to *my* home.

The time is short, two months at my disposal to tour the country. I know the land from descriptions in books, but these paled in comparison to that which I saw with my own eyes. Such a beauty I have until now never encountered anywhere else, though I have traveled widely. It seems to me that the sky here is bluer than anywhere else and the Mediterranean reflects the blueness and radiates beauty all around.

I spend most of my time in Haifa, a port city which sits on a mountain facing Mount Carmel, dipped in green and flowers creating a dreamlike picture especially at night, when it reflects the sea like thousands of crystals. The environment is so splendid that I cannot avert my gaze. I visit the Persian garden with exotic palms, plants and

---

56   The Five Books of Moses.
57   Homey.

flowers, *mamesh*[58] a *Gan-Eden*[59] of beauty in this world. The city of Haifa pulses with life and laughter. Every day, new ships arrive with *olim*,[60] tourists and merchants. One hears many languages, but mostly Hebrew.

Israel: A small country but with a large perspective on all aspects of life, an equal to the most powerful countries.

Every city and village that I encounter could merit its own history, but for this I would have to write many articles, and it would take much time and patience from the readers. I will try to limit my words and make this as short as possible.

Now I am in Acco, a city near Haifa. It was once exclusively an Arab city, but now it was rebuilt in the most modern style. The sea is hypnotic there. It is difficult to leave. I spend whole days there on the coast, playing in the waves. The sun warms and burns my body, everywhere the noise of children's laughter and play.

From there I travel to Tel Aviv, a modern, industrial city with a large cultural center, the Habima theater, national opera, and uncountable theaters and movie houses. Multi-story buildings are constantly being built; the city is burgeoning in every corner with work, trade, and noise. In the evenings it is difficult to find an open seat in the outdoor cafes, so characteristic of the Orient. People are laughing, talking politics and philosophizing. Every day I visit new places, each one prettier than the previous one.

I complete a three day journey through the Negev desert, an unbelievable panorama. It is impossible to transmit the level of beauty. The colorful mountains with multicolored sand hug the desert. It is no longer just a desert of sand and stones but a chain of blooming fields and gardens. They are building, watering, and planting more and more, and all of this is done by Jewish hands (we have always been accused of incompetence at working the land). Jews are standing by the ploughs, hammer in hand, working with love. The knowledge that they are building their own country energizes them. I am a

---

58 Used in this context to mean literally.
59 Garden of Eden or Paradise.
60 Literally meaning "going up," it is a term used to denote individuals who move to Israel.

bit ashamed that I am not one of the pioneers contributing to the building of the Jewish home.

The bus cuts through the mountains and valleys, where new paths and highways were built. The beautiful desert city Be'er Sheva with modern amenities calls out far and wide tearing off pieces of the Negev and plants there blooming gardens. We approach the southern port city of Eilat, which borders three Arab countries.

Traveling through the Gulf of Aqaba with boats that have glass floors, a whole world is discovered of colorful fish and plants. One cannot forget these impressions that were so lively and fresh.

We visit many places that are mentioned in the Torah- The copper mines of *Shlomo Hamelekh*[61] and the potash ditches of *Avrom Avinu*[62] in Sodom. We see before us the image of Lot's wife in salt at the Dead Sea. The water here is thick with minerals and keeps us at the surface, even when we aren't swimming. We stop at a waterfall in Ein Gedi, which shines with rainbow colors - a fantastic picture!

From time to time, we encounter Bedouins in the desert, who contrast strongly with what we have seen, with their clothing and primitive dwellings, and with the camels walking in the sand. We travel through Ashkelon, where a troop of resting soldiers greets us. We hear in their songs the pride that they take in being part of a Jewish army.

The next day, I am already on a train to the holy city of Jerusalem. We ride very close to the Jordanian border. My gaze falls on the other side and how different it is on the Jordanian side than the Israeli side. I want to stay longer; there is so much to see.

Jerusalem is a spectacular city surrounded by mountains and gardens and every corner sings the glory and the greatness of the Jewish people. It enlivens the whole history of our people, the center of God's house, the *Beis Hamikdash,*[63] and the important role of Zion.

We visit Mount Zion, from where we can see the whole city. There lies the grave of *Dovid Hamelekh.*[64] We go through the pilgrims

---

[61] King Solomon.

[62] The Patriarch Abraham.

[63] The Holy Temple in Jerusalem.

[64] King David.

courtyard and find the room where people light candles in memory of Dovid Hamelekh.

At *Yad Vashem*[65] we go through the room where the memory of our martyrs is sanctified. Ash is brought from the five most gruesome concentration camps where one third of our nation was tortured and murdered. We also found there plaques with the names of every destroyed settlement. Our dear shtetele Kremenitz was also eternalized with a plaque. My heart cries and bleeds looking at the plaque.

On the way to Herzl's grave, we pass graves of young people, almost children, who gave up their lives in the struggle for the Jewish homeland. The spectacular Hebrew University, with dozens of departments and laboratories, is a center for higher education and culture, maybe the best one in the whole Middle East, the Hadassah Hospital and more and more . . .

We also visit Meah Shearim, where the most extremely religious people dwell. Time is running out and I want to catch more of the beauty of the land. Bnei Brak, Petach Tikva, *kibbutzim*,[66] *yishuvim*,[67] each one with its own unique lifestyle. We visit several archaeological sites. We find ourselves in Caesaria, where they discovered whole Roman cities, with palaces that recall the culture of 1,000 years into the past. I don't miss out on the Galil. We pass through so many towns and villages, it is hard to list all of the names. Like on a screen, pictures of nature and beauty run past my eyes; the romantic Kinneret, which inspired so many poets to produce heartfelt songs of beauty and love. My gaze falls upon the Hula Valley, and it looks like a carpet of various colors, fields and man-made rivers for raising fish. A dream, a dream for me and I want to hold onto it as long as I can, but I must come to the epilogue, the peak of my trip to Israel. This was my presence at the Kremenitz memorial ceremony in Tel Aviv. My brother had told me about the memorial ceremonies that take place every year in Tel Aviv, to which almost all of the Kremenitzers in Israel flock from every corner of the country. However much one works in the kibbutz, the village or the city, everyone feels the holy obligation to give time to remember and to honor the memory of our

---

[65]   Holocaust memorial museum in Jerusalem established in 1953.
[66]   Socialist collectives.
[67]   Jewish settlements.

dear Kremenitz, whose life was prematurely cut off so gruesomely by the German and Ukrainian murderers.

All bring their Israeli-born children and grandchildren who, though they never saw Kremenitz, were implanted with a love for our dear, beautiful and never to be forgotten shtetele. There is a nice culture house named after our long dead noble and learned Ber Levinsohn. The walls are decorated with photographs and panoramas of Kremenitz and pictures taken during the Holocaust; everything is guarded with love and memory for generations. A fund is collected of donations from every Kremenitzer in Israel and from many other countries around the world for whom Kremenitz is so dear. The fund will eternalize the memory of the Kremenitzer martyrs through the golden book.

Many people in their speeches mention our brother Wachman, who supports the project with a full hand, both materially and spiritually. Wachman shows not only a deep interest in their work (which should be all of our work), but also much love and heartfelt conviction and is always ready to help and encourage whenever necessary.

I can hardly believe that it is real. I found myself in a world that I had thought was a vanished one. I barely entered the meeting place and I was suddenly enveloped with a warm and *heimish* atmosphere. I was surrounded on all sides by people so glad to see me. I was so moved that I could hardly speak a word the first few minutes. Tears of joy filled my heart. I felt like I was at home on the Dubner Rogetke and, like once upon a time, I see around me all of my friends from youth, with whom I spent my childhood, playing and learning in the same school.

Oh, all were so dear to me in this moment, like brothers and sisters. Here and there, I met neighbors from the older generation, and like one big family, we all rejoiced together.

I could recount so much about the meeting, but it would be too much at one time. With much attentiveness, I listened to the speeches of our honored and learned Kremenitzers. I was most moved by the reading of the wonderful writings of our beloved and talented brother Rapapport. Brother Rapapport is in constant contact with

every Kremenitzer *farband*[68] wherever he is, be it in Israel, Argentina or America, and supports them financially and with his spiritual work and heartfelt songs and descriptions of our shtetele. He encourages, calls, wakes, and empowers every Kremenitzer to create and to contribute to the building of the huge memorial of our beloved Kremenitz. Unfortunately, he runs into so many obstacles, but he does not give up and struggles for the ultimate victory (so help him God). I was asked to give him a personal regards and a "thanks for your work" and again a "please do not give up, do even more." The time comes for me to say goodbye to my newfound friends. I would so much like to hold onto the moment hugging all of them and never forget them but, sadly, we must part.

Full of rich and unforgettable impressions do I leave Israel. I saw a lot here, traveled the length and breadth of the land, but something else remains for me to see when I will once again come. I throw my last glance from the plane, which raises itself up to fly back. All of a sudden, I deeply long for those beautiful nights, and I thank God for allowing me to actualize my dream and visit the Jewish homeland for which my heart is now filled with unlimited love.

After my first trip to Israel, I finally was able to start replacing horrid memories with beautiful visuals of this most exquisite land. In the dear town of Acco, I remember its beautiful surroundings of lush trees and flowers. I can still feel the cool and pleasant breeze from the sea in the stillness of the hot summer nights and the splashing of the warm weather waves from the Mediterranean. On the clear sandy beach I see displays of colors from the beautiful sun of Israel. I am looking forward to the next time I visit again. Everything in life comes unexpectedly and I just have to hope and wait for the best. There will be a time when I return to my beautiful land of Israel and my happiness will be fulfilled. In the meantime, I have to work hard to build my happy future.

---

[68] Yiddish for alliance or association member.

Elza, Kuba and Helen

Kuba and Helen, Mounts of Upper Galilee

| Chapter Fifteen |

ROUGH TIMES

*L*ife in Brooklyn was not easy. The family had settled in a mouse infested railroad apartment in Brownsville, that included a living room, kitchen, two bedrooms and a bathroom. The neighbors looked down upon the new European immigrants as if they came from a backwards country. Once, a neighbor asked my grandmother if she ever saw a tomato before. Ironically, it was my grandmother who was far more educated and sophisticated than the local Brooklyn residents.

My grandmother went to school at night to receive her high school equivalency diploma so that she could work as a nurse. She would sew clothing on the side for extra money while she studied. My grandfather, Jack, opened an electrical surplus store in which he repaired generators, transformers, and other electrical equipment. Business was tough and the neighborhood was dangerous.

At one point, in the 1960s while living in Bensonhurst, my grandfather was robbed at gunpoint, ordered to undress and was tied up as the thieves ran away with his hard earned money. He was forced to pay off the mob so that they would ensure his protection. My father recalls coming home from school that day and finding his father in bed, beaten and bruised.

In the summers, my grandmother would go with my father and uncle to the Catskill Mountains, where she worked as a nurse. My grandfather remained working in the city and would come up to visit on weekends. The summers in the city were unbearable and he would sleep out on the

fire escape because there was no air conditioning in the apartment. Despite these sacrifices, the family was slowly adjusting to their new home and my grandmother was beginning to make friends and feel fulfilled again working as a nurse.

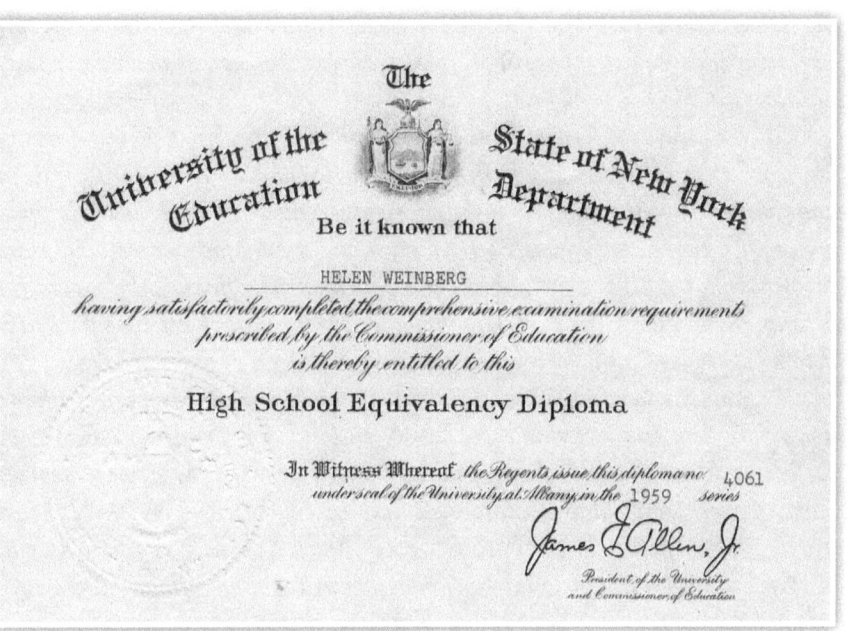

Diploma received at age 45

Then in 1967, Kuba suffered a heart attack. He was sick for several months with a heart condition before he passed away in April of 1967. My grandmother was working as a nurse at Maimonides Hospital in Brooklyn, New York at the time. As a result of her brother's illness she became very depressed and could no longer work. Outwardly, she tried to keep the appearance of normalcy but the war destroyed her in many ways and the loss of her only brother was the final straw.

This was a very difficult time for the family. My grandmother was not able to socialize with friends nor was she able to carry out daily activities with ease. The family doctor, a native Pole, evaluated her and determined she was indeed suffering from severe depression and not fit to work. She attempted to get reparations from Germany for her ill health but was unsuccessful.

At the age of 23, my father, Bernard, was concerned about leaving his mother as he planned for his first trip to Israel. Years of depression and unemployment followed my grandmother into the early 1970s when my grandfather finally insisted that she open a knitting and sewing store in Bensonhurst. The store, unfortunately, was not financially successful because in her kind nature, my grandmother spent much of her time patiently helping customers with their sewing questions instead of making sales.

Despite the hardships my grandparents endured, they created a loving home for their two sons and did an exceptional job in raising them. My father and uncle excelled academically, both earning bachelor's degrees from Cooper Union and doctorate degrees in engineering- my father from Polytechnic Institute of New York University in aerospace engineering and my uncle from Princeton University in aeronautical engineering.

March 4, 1967

To Whom It May Concern: Re: Helen Weinberg
                              2033 78th Street
                              Brooklyn, New York

Mrs. Helen Weinberg has been under my medical care
since June 1950.

Patient stated that during the German occupation during
World War II, her hometown was occupied by the Germans.
Patient had to leave her hometown. She went to Russia.
In Russia she was deported to Siberia. Patient suffered
extreme hardships due to inadequate, improper, andinsuff-
icient food, clothing, and shelter; forced to live in
a severe climate which she could not adjust to; forced
to perform hard labor.

Under my medical care, patient is being treated for:

Severe anxiety neurosis with depressive reaction with
the following symptoms: headaches, dizziness, nausea,
vomitting, pains in the chest, palpitation of the heart,
abdominal cramps, attacks of diarrheas, insomnia,
lack of ambition, inability to socialize or seek pleasure,
periods of depressed moods, weak and faint spells,

Hyperthyroidism(toxic diffuse goiter). A few years ago
patient had radioactive iodine. Patient also developed
pre-tibial mixed edema proven by biopsy. Patient is
very nervous;has tremors of the hands, palpitation of
heart, Exopthalmos, profuse sweating, fatigue, loss of
weight without loss of appetite, irritable, emotional
outbursts, can not control her temper, very often patient
has difficulty in swallowing, hoarseness.

Because of the poor physical and mental condition of this
patient, her earning capacity is diminished by seventy
percent.

It is my opinion that the hardships and privations endured
by this patient have produced the abovementioned conditions.

Patient states that prior to her confinement, she
enjoyed good, normal health.
                            Very truly yours,

JD/jed   JACOB DAMASHEK, M.D.

In 1980, my grandparents closed both their businesses and moved to West Hartford, Connecticut to be closer to my family.

In West Hartford, my grandparents lived just a short mile away from the home where I grew up. I was fortunate enough to have shared many wonderful events with them such as birthday parties, dance recitals, Jewish holidays and, of course, our yearly Thanksgiving dinners - their tribute to coming to America. Although I was aware that my grandmother was never fully able to enjoy life, she did receive great comfort and happiness from her grandchildren. We were her "pride and joy" as she would say. She remained living in West Hartford until she passed away in 1997.

Chapter Sixteen

WORDS ARE NO LONGER ENOUGH

Eulogy by my father, Bernard Weinberg

September 28, 1997

Last night a very special person was taken from us, the last of her family in her generation. She was a devoted wife and a loving mother and grandmother. But she was much more than that. You probably knew her as a reserved, quiet and frail woman. But you really didn't know her at all.

I will tell you a little bit about her. She was a fighter who wouldn't quit. We thank *Hashem*[69] for allowing us to have had her all this while during her deepening illness. We also thank *Hashem* that she went peacefully, without pain, and near her family in her home. To the very end she was concerned about my father's health, about the welfare of her children and grandchildren and also how she was going to bake a honey cake for Rosh Hashanah. To our great joy and surprise, my sister-in-law Susan brought with her a honey cake that my mother made before her illness that lay frozen in Washington. Mom, if you can hear us, we will have your honey cake this year.

However, she was engulfed with a much different deeper pain that has lasted more than 50 years. Last Friday night I stayed the night

---

[69] The colloquial Hebrew word used for God.

with my mother. As she went in and out of her sleep she kept saying I will never forget, I will never forget. She can now finally rest.

If you would see pictures of her in her youth you would have seen a beautiful, carefree person, an athlete who excelled in the broad jump. But the pictures after the war show a very different person. She was born in the small Polish town of Kremenitz, during the War to end all wars, a town known as the birth place of Isaac Stern, the great violinist. There she developed her love for learning, being surrounded by an extended family of lawyers, doctors, university professors and *talmidei chachomim.*[70]

Her talents were many faceted. Although it was not generally accepted in those years, she studied in Krakow and fulfilled her dream of becoming a nurse. But her hands could perform magic, sewing, knitting, crocheting and needlepoint. I cherish and still wear the sweaters she made me. But those were not all of her talents. She was a poet and a writer in both Polish and Yiddish. She had mastered other languages as well, and Aaron and I still recall the lullaby in French she would sing to us. Her hand writing was artistic yet precise, and she was neat, a trait I am sure my eldest daughter inherited.

The Holocaust changed her. She suffered through Siberia, prison, hunger and poverty and lost almost her entire family. That pain she would never forget.

But she was a fighter who wouldn't quit. And today she is survived by two sons, and six grandchildren, two of whom have married.

It is strange what thoughts are brought to the surface at a time like this. But this is the way I remember my mother. She introduced me to art and bought me my first paint by number set. She introduced me to jigsaw puzzles, stamp collecting, Yiddish music, and of course, books. She would squirrel away money, and we did not have much at that time, so I could buy photography equipment, painting supplies and books. Speaking of books, at the beginning of the school year she would help me cover my books using paper bags, not with cool book covers that my friends had. I was embarrassed then, but if I never admitted it, Mom, your way was better.

She helped us with our homework, drew maps for us and taught me how to knit for my fraternity initiation. Oh, the sandwiches she

---

[70] Individuals who are Talmud scholars.

made us for lunch so we wouldn't go hungry. And, yet against her better judgment, she allowed us to buy comic books and we had a pretty good collection.

She showed unconditional love. After Eileen and I were engaged, Eileen noticed a gray hair on my head. We confronted my mother and, without skipping a beat, without looking at my head, with a straight face she remarked, "Not my Bernishu."

She loved games of knowledge. More recently it was *Jeopardy*, but in the late 50's it was *The $64,000 Question*. She wanted to be on the show so she studied the life of her hero Louis Pasteur and sent in a letter to try to become a contestant. Although she wasn't chosen, her search for knowledge never abated.

And she sacrificed by working second jobs so we would have a Jewish education, a legacy Aaron and I have passed down to our children. What would we have been without her?

The pain is gone now Mom. Your memory and love will always be with us.

Weinberg Family 1981

Eulogy by my brother, Rabbi Dr. Noam Weinberg

September 28, 1997

In a little over a week or so, on the holiday of Yom Kippur, we will be saying the *tefilla*[71] of the *Asara Harugei Malchut*.[72] The episode is told of the great sage Rabbi Channina the son of Tradyon who was burned alive because he resisted the Roman edict against teaching Torah. As he was dying, he exclaimed, "The parchment of the holy Torah is burning but the letters are flying up to heaven." The Kloisenberg Rebbe explains that this is the banner which we Jews hold high. The other nations of the world may break us physically, but our spirit can never be destroyed!

While the Jews traveled with the *Mishkan*[73] it held the first set of tablets that Moshe broke. The Jewish people were careful to bring it with them wherever they went to show specifically that physically the Jewish people are like anyone else. However, spiritually we have a special connection with *Hashem*.

All throughout Jewish history it has been this way. We have been murdered, ridiculed, beaten and starved but we have never been silenced. My *Bobby, Yenta Bas Baruch Chaim,*[74] was a living testimony of that. Her life was not easy, to say the least, having lost her parents, sisters, brothers-in-law, extended family and friends to the Nazis. She was imprisoned for almost two years in a Russian jail, beaten and broken. Afterwards she was sent to a Russian labor camp in Siberia. Following her liberation, she met my grandfather and soon married. Her body might have been broken but her spirit remained very much alive. She continued to raise a Jewish family in Samarkand, then Germany and then New York. It is the merit of my *Bobby* that there

---

71   Prayer.

72   The ten martyrs who were murdered as a result of openly observing and teaching the Torah during the time of the Roman persecutions of Israel in the second century.

73   Tabernacle.

74   My grandmother's Hebrew name.

are eight holy souls in this world, carrying with us wherever we go a piece of my *Bobby* in our hearts.

Even at the end of her life, my *Bobby* was still hoping and awaiting the final redemption, as she asked me on Friday "When is *Moshiach*[75] coming?" This was my *Bobby*. A woman who exemplified the words of the *Rambam*[76] in his thirteen principles of faith, "I believe with perfect faith in the coming of the Moshiach."

Even though it was difficult seeing the destruction of European Jewry, my grandmother's belief remained rock solid.

So what do we do now? We engrave the sacred memory of our mother, grandmother and friend in our lives and strengthen our own commitment to Torah and our belief in God. We do this so that *Bobby* can look down on us and say, "My life was not in vain, I survived the destruction for a reason."

We are the reason! Our commitment to the Torah and its commandments is the reason. And it should be in this merit that the soul of my *Bobby* has an easy transition into the world to come where she will look down and be proud and smile and say that it was all worth it!

May she serve as a spiritual guide for all of us.

---

[75] The Jewish Messiah.

[76] Rabbi Moshe Ben Maimon (Maimonides), one of the most famous Jewish commentators, 1138-1204.

Weinberg Family, 1988, at my brother Noam's Bar Mitzvah

There are those who pass on and leave behind a fortune - an inheritance abundant with money and jewels. And then there are those that pass on and leave behind a legacy.

Bobby is survived by two sons, six grandchildren and nineteen great grandchildren, all of whom are Torah observant and value the Jewish tradition with sincerity and conviction. Bobby paved the way for our family by striving to improve the world in which she lived. She overcame extreme obstacles with her strong will and love for her family. Bobby will never know the difference she made in this world and how many people she inspired throughout her life . . . and after. Helen Weinberg nee Gun achieved so much, yet with so little. I hope I can raise my family with the same dignity and respect that she did. Bobby was the true matriarch of the Weinberg family and her legacy will surely live on.

Me, age 8, with my Bobby

ASSORTED POETRY

(Translated from the original Yiddish)

By Helen Weinberg

TICK TOCK

This sound is known to everyone. Even a child hearing this sound knows that this is the striking of a clock, the movement of time.

A clock hanging on a wall or a watch which is bound on the wrist or placed in a pocket is a marvelous mechanism. The inventor should be praised for his ingenious creation.

The clock is the measure of time running day and night through seasons and years while myriads of centuries elapse. The clock conducts our life while we depend on it.

The instrument to measure time has been with us for several thousand years.
The ancient Egyptians had a sun dial which guided their lives.

Today we can't imagine life without a clock, a wonder and, at the same time, a big dictator.

Whether we like it or not, we must bow to it. Otherwise we are lost in time.

From birth until death people depend on the clock. It divides our day and night. According to it we rise in the morning and retire to sleep at night.

With the sign of the clock, we begin and complete our work.

I saw people dying and, in the last minute of their life, they asked me the time. Would it have made any difference if it was four o'clock in the morning or seven o'clock at night?

One wants to know for sure in that moment of dying when the clock decreed his death.

When we are happy, we want time to pass by slowly. In times of hardships we want the time to speed up but the clock is laughing at us as if to say, "I am the boss and you have to listen to me."

When we grow older we want time to go back so we may relive our younger days, but we can't. Time, like life, can never be recalled.

The clock is one of the greatest necessities of life but at the same time it is evil to us. Running without interruption, it carries away our life.

TSU MUTERS TOG - TO MOTHER'S DAY

To you, O mother,
This day is dedicated.
With praise and song,
You are celebrated.
For one day, my love,
You are a queen.
Your crown shimmering
With radiance and diamonds.
You are brought gifts
with woven flowers.
You are extolled with honor
Loved and respected.
For one day of the year,
You are dignified and dear,
Great and distinguished,
None more loyal.
But, who can appreciate you?
My *mameleh*,[77] my life?
Your greatness and beauty
The strength of your efforts.
God implanted in you,
A heart full of love,
Unbound and mighty,
Every day, hour of life.
For your child you will run,
Into flames of a fire.
Your life you'd give up,
For your child is so dear to you.
Forever on your mind,
Is the best for your children,
A caress and a comfort,
You always accomplish wonders.
How many times in despair,
When there is no way out in sight,

---

77   Mother

You will seek and discover,
And find the solution.
When your child has a fever,
You stay awake worrying,
You comfort, refresh him,
Like dew in the morning.
So your love is gigantic,
Deep in your heart,
People wander for years
Seeking such a wonder.
Incomparable is your love.
Patient, consistent,
Until the last day of life.
You can keep it well hidden.
Poets sing of you,
You inspire artists and painters,
Major works have been created
All from your great love.
On behalf of your children,
You are pained and insulted,
With a tear and a sigh of longing,
Your love is eternal.
O, how delighted you all are,
To be a beloved mother,
Life blossoms, sings and rejoices,
Illuminating your days.
I was also once happy,
My life flowed in bright blue springtime,
Sang in joy, full of melodies.
My heart delighted in the mirth
I loved so much
My dear mother,
Her delicate gaze, it rests forever.
I had thought, naive and childlike,
My mother must, she'll live forever.
I will forever love my mother,
Not forgetting her bright being.
She lit up my path,

Inspired me to strive high.
When she passed so tragically terribly
I lost my way in life.
Around me I felt emptiness,
Without sound, color or purpose.
A mother is to everyone's knowledge,
The source of love and way of life,
Not to forget for even a day,
God's gift to love forever.
The span of life,
It pushes and hurries.
The world around is full of wonder,
The greatest however,
Is a mother.
Her great love,
For her children.

Rochele Gun

MIT FREYD UN FARGENIGN -
WITH JOY AND PLEASURE

The river is gurgling,
It plays and makes waves,
Flirts with the sunshine,
And rainbow colors.
The flowers are dancing,
So pleasant and colored,
The hills in the distance,
They wink and they call out,
It's springtime, it's springtime,
A world of nuances!
The spring is to youth
Very fitting,
It wakes up, enlivens.
The scene is fantastic.
It's blooming with fragrance
Like the roses in the garden.
It sings free of worry
Like the birds in the air.
Also my youth,
Returns with the spring,
Overjoyed is my heart,
Full with rays of the sun.
It caresses and comforts.
Exalted and happy,
Is beautiful youth
That springtime is here.

Helen, 1948

DI BADAYTUNG FUN LIBE - THE MEANING OF LOVE

God has, with love
created the world,
And has out of love
Given it to man.
And all that which blossoms
And all that which lives
With beauty, with love
It is honored.
You see how the flowers,
Bloom in the field,
Take on beauty,
Grow and spread out.
With splendor and radiance
They fill up the air,
For God has His power
with love infused.
And flowers that blossom
In the garden by the house,
How delightful they shine
In color and size.
They have a life
And they have a sparkle.
For with love and with life
Has a hand planted them.
Trees you will plant
With love and care,
Fruit they will give you
Delicious and delightful.
They feel your love
Your delicate hand,
Like a living vase
That can understand.
And you wander around,
And you hear the singing
And the nature, it plays,

Full of love's sounds.
And the deep night,
The woods deep in thought,
You hear nightingales singing,
Full of love do they sound.
Life is so sweet,
And life is so rich,
When love is present
in such a life.
Love creates greatness
And love creates beauty
And whatever your struggle,
It can only be achieved through love.

Helen and Jack, 1950s

FRILING - SPRING

The spring is anxious,
He runs and hurries.
He knows that his power is short.
For soon he will have to,
His crown to concede,
But the work of the spring,
Is so hard to complete,
Just now not too long,
The winter did rule.
From his throne and his power,
Wanted not to depart.
Here and there he has flung,
Snow and wind in his struggle
To lengthen the battle as much as he can.
With gladness does nature,
Welcome the spring,
She smiles, she beams.
The sun in the heavens,
The forest is ringing
With song and with laughter,
Splendid and pretty
Is the full of his bloom.

Helen, 1960s

TSUZAMEN - TOGETHER

This poem was written in honor of Helen and Jack Weinberg's 25th
Wedding Anniversary

Together, beloved, together
Moving forward together in life.
So happy we are together
When light and dignity are here.
A fourth of a century passed
I remember the moment so clear
You came to me, my most beloved,
A new life began to blossom.
So fresh I can see it before me,
Never forget it, shall I.
When abandoned, lonely and broken
In the world like a valley of darkness
Like a ship that's been damaged by waves,
Cast by the stormy sea.
Alone, I stood by the helm,
There was no one to help me at all.
And the heavens covered in clouds,
Heavy, black, impenetrable,
And the sun, trapped behind them,
Vicious winds blowing cold.
The winds pursued my small ship,
Into the distant and infinite sea
Feeding my miserable loneliness,
Progressively weakening me.
My willpower's completely been spent,
Far from my home and my loved ones,
Weak from hunger, depression, and loneliness
A nightmarish world of despair.
I am about to lose hold of the helm,
In my struggle with the powerful sea.
I'll be swallowed by the waves,
Smothered by furious clouds.
Then you came to me, O my beloved,

And you quickly took over the helm,
You didn't let my ship sink,
You didn't allow the waves to swallow me.
Suddenly, a ray of sunlight appeared,
The clouds in the sky moved aside,
And the wind slowed its speed
And the waves silenced their roar.
We swam, you and I together
Through the difficult waves of our lives,
Wandered through mountains and valleys.
You awakened my hope and my striving.
Light shone more and more in my life,
You wiped the tears from my eyes,
And guarded me from every danger,
Didn't allow worry, despair.
You believed in a brighter tomorrow,
A new life will blossom for us,
When together we emerge as the victors,
From the bitter and terrible struggle.
Since then, years have passed,
Rhythmically moving along,
Hand in hand, we stride together,
With love, loyalty and dignity.
We feel so happy together,
Like the springtime, blooming and singing,
Full of sunshine, flowers and herbs,
Full of joy for our accomplishments.
Far away have the waves carried,
Those days of aloneness and pain,
Now our paths and our lives are shining,
Like a clean and colorful rainbow.

Helen and Jack, 1968

LID FUN LIBEH - ODE TO LOVE

When you give your child love,
Your goal is achieved.
It will feel the love,
And the gift is enriched.
It will grow and mature,
And will reach more light,
It will pursue greater knowledge,
And will bring you more joy.
If only people understood,
How great is the value,
Of love's flames
Which makes pleasant the world.
Then generation upon generations,
Would bring to the world
So much grandeur
Full of heavenly delight.
Not with hate or with blood,
Can one rule the world.
But with love and with virtue,
Is power worthwhile.
Nations have fallen,
Disappeared from the world
Absent in these cases,
Was love's supreme law.
Often a person,
Gets lost deep in the woods,
Among beasts and webs,
When it's terrible and cold,
And he suffers greatly,
From the wolves and the lions,
He cannot ask for help.
But the truth in life,
Is eternal, from God,
That with love and with loving,
You reach the secret.
The love, the love,

Which is holy and high,
Which the wolf and the tiger,
He intuits, he smells it.
He won't take your life,
He won't draw your blood,
For your weapon is love,
Your weapon is goodness.
If the artist for his art,
Lacked a sense of love,
His work wouldn't have any value,
Greatness it wouldn't possess.
With love for writing,
Are books composed,
With love for people,
Have cures been discovered.
Only with love, with love
Will you take the world.
Only with love's power
Will the world shine with beauty.
Godly love,
Is powerful and beautiful,
We can this love
Reach on our own.

Helen with her two sons Aaron and Bernard, 1960s

DER HAYNT IZ DO - TODAY IS HERE

Today is here,
Accept it with joy,
Worries are gone
From yesterday's suffering.
Yesterday is gone,
You can't bring it back,
Its purpose no more,
Than to ponder its meaning.
Today is here,
Fill it up with beauty,
So much you can do,
Crowning him with glory.
You messed up yesterday,
Sunken in worry,
Much time have you spent,
Thinking about tomorrow.
But tomorrow is now,
Bring life into him,
New goals, new friends,
Will today give to you.
Don't wait for tomorrow,
For today is here now,
You can't worry forever
For yesterday's gone.
Love today,
Love your life,
The greatest gift,
God has granted mankind.
Be good to people,
Love them without hesitation,
Important are only people,
Don't think just of things.
Again will today,
Come and stand,
The eternal friend,
For today is beautiful.

Helen and Jack, 1960

TROYMEN - DREAMS

Every person sometimes likes to dream,
To tear himself away from the real world.
And he escapes to the upper realms,
Where beauty love and pleasure abound.
When you are devastated by suffering and misery,
With no way out, lost and in grief,
Turn your thoughts away to the dreams
And they can also be your comfort.
You spend your whole life on stones
Among the noise and the sounds of work.
Let yourself go swing from the trees,
Feel the softness of moss and of satin.
There's much you can do while you are dreaming,
far in your wandering thoughts.
In palatial rooms you can dwell,
With servants and glittering gems
For you strive so hard for your goals,
You move slowly, the struggle is hard
It's advised that you let yourself dream,
Dreams will lighten the burden.
In your dreams run away to your youth,
It is full with melodies, with nuance,
Live through the wonder of youth,
Every moment is joy and pleasure.
The times cannot be brought back,
Beloved moments of life
However in dreams they are yours,
To take and renew for eternity.

Helen and Jack, 1980s

DI OYGN - THE EYES

Wonderfully beautiful is the world around us,
pretty colors and shades
sometimes delightfully singing
It is hard to avert one's eyes.
These eyes can see so much,
The priceless gift for mankind
So important are eyes.
For they are the mirror of the heart.
There are so many kinds of eyes,
the colors the shapes and emotions
Nations can be recognized by their eyes,
A picture of a person's character.
Eyes of black, like golden coals
Eyes of brown, tinted and filled with colors,
Eyes of blue, with the color of the sky
Bursting with delight and beauty
Eyes of grey and of green,
Wide open, clear and kind.
Mirroring the environment,
With its flowers, streams and skies.
There are also very pale eyes,
Like water flooding the banks,
As if tired, eternally shut,
Without meaning without emotion.
The form of these thousands of eyes,
Diverse among so many people,
Straight eyes . . . .

Helen and Jack, 1990s

CHANUKAH LIKHTELEKH - HANNUKAH LIGHTS

Full of light the night is sparkling,
Shimmered have the Chanukah candles.
So delightfully have they illuminated
The deep, snowy night.
O, little Chanukah candles,
How much greatness dwells in you,
For it is *yontif*,[78] Chanukah-*yontif*
Which bears with it miracles.
As I look deeply into the little candles,
I see the image as if it was yesterday.
In my shtetele it is now Chanukah
So the candles shine, it is happy and beautiful.
And the snow falls deeper and deeper,
It has covered everything in sight.
And my shtetele is enchanted with a coat of snow
Waking the muses of sleep.
I feel the mood of the Chanukah *yontif*,
Surrounded by joy, dance, and song.
We run to play with *dreydlekh*[79] and cards
Father gives everyone gifts.
It's my youth, the blossoming years,
The poetic years of life.
Never to be forgotten,
They can always be brought back to life.
Grandpa sits snuggled in the corner,
I am the first to run to him,
"O, tell me *Zeydenyu*,[80] dear,
of the heroes of Jewish past!"
I listen enraptured, to the stories,
I swallow his every word
About the mighty Maccabees,
Who exalted the Jewish people.

---

[78] The Yiddish way of referring to certain Jewish holidays.
[79] Plural of dreydl, a four-sided spinning top.
[80] Endearing term to reference a grandfather.

Great miracles happened then,
Our land was in grave danger.
The *Beis Hamikdash*[81] defiled
Close to 3,000 years ago.
And a great miracle happened,
A small pitcher burned for eight days
Instead of the 1 day's worth it had,
And the Jewish faith won again.

---

[81] The Holy Temple in Jerusalem.

Helen and Jack, 1995

www.ingramcontent.com/pod-product-compliance
Lightning Source LLC
Chambersburg PA
CBHW061259280526
45784CB00002B/822